WVL

£2·50

Eventing

Eventing

Judith Campbell

Photographs by Srdja Djukanovic

Arthur Barker Limited
London
A subsidiary of Weidenfeld (Publishers) Limited

Published in Great Britain by Arthur Barker Limited
11 St John's Hill, London SW11

ISBN 0 213 16613 5

Filmset by Keyspools, Limited, Golborne, Lancs.
Printed in Great Britain by
Butler & Tanner Limited, Frome.

Contents

The British team at Kiev
Sue Hatherly weighing in at Ledyard
Alison Oliver with her son.

PHOTOGRAPHS BY SRDJA DJUKANOVIC
Picture editor : Julia Brown

List of Illustrations

Introduction

You can call it eventing or horse trials. In France it still sometimes goes by the old term of the *militaire*, but is now generally known as the *concours complet d'equitation*, a self-explanatory name that translates into the conveniently abbreviated 'combined training'. The sport comes in two forms, each appealing to a different standard of horsemanship and horse, but whatever the title, whatever the grade, this is a sport that concerns the all-rounder as opposed to the specialist, and no other type of equestrian competition ensures such a systematic and complete training of rider and horse.

The three-day events that are at the top and the one-day trials that concern the lower stratas but are the backbone of the sport, are very different facets of combined training but they are both based on the same three phases.

The first of these phases is a dressage test. Dressage is a creative art with a functional purpose. It is a form of training, but a well-performed test is a fluid and graceful 'ballet' of the horse. Provided that it does not actually 'blow up' in the arena, any horse capable of doing the other phases of an event can do the required standard of dressage. At Olympic level some of the paces and figures required are those 'airs on the ground' once considered in England as the province only of the foreign *manège* rider concentrating on *haute école*. They are in fact the first steps towards the dramatic and immensely difficult 'airs above the ground', originating in the natural leaps of stallions fighting and horses at play, that were part of the offensive and defensive training of the ancient war horse. Today the 'airs above the ground' are an ingredient of the pure, classical horsemanship, developed as a fine art during the Renaissance, and now taught and demonstrated only at the Spanish School in Vienna.

Dressage, also of classical purity, again without the 'airs above the ground', but progressing to standards far beyond the requirements of eventing, is a sport on its own, gaining in popularity even in the jet age. However, because of the skill and years of training involved at this level, it is more likely to remain the province of the talented few. The dressage tests given in eventing are graded in relation to the type of competition and classes included in a particular trial. Basically the horses are required to be supple, balanced, and obedient to the aids. This training on the flat, once correctly understood and applied, is of benefit to every type of riding horse and pony.

Largely owing to a different interpretation of the meaning of dressage a certain amount of controversy has always surrounded this phase in an event. The rules of the Olympic three-day event dressage test were revised two years before the 1936 Olympic Games, on the initiative of the Italians, who belonged to the Caprilli school of thought that believes in allowing the horse to perform almost on its own. They argued that a horse trained to maintain a high-necked, over-collected position and taught to move with exaggerated impulsion, could not be expected to 'use' itself effectively on its own initiative when sudden trouble arises on the cross-country course. This is not a true picture of the horse trained correctly in elementary dressage but the Italians demonstrated to the FEI with dressage based on little more than a test of the basic obedience of a horse in its naturally balanced position, and won their point. It was agreed that the phase would in future be judged, not so much on correct collection, as on the horse's willingness to execute the required movements calmly, readily, obediently, without anticipation or delay, and with sufficient impulsion only to assure the cadenced beat and rhythm of the gaits.

This form of test divorced even Olympic combined training dressage from Grand Prix dressage, but owing to the war the 1940 and 1944 Olympics were not held, and the majority of the European countries did not participate in the limited Games of 1948. By 1952 the majority of the 'reformers' had faded away, and at subsequent Olympics the requirements of the dressage phase once more included collection and resembled a less exacting test of 'pure' dressage. Largely through more commonly using the term 'training on the flat' instead of 'dressage', a satisfactory compromise has now emerged. In recent years the term 'working paces' has been substituted for the former 'collected paces' in dressage tests used in eventing, and the top-class riders of the world continue to demonstrate that a horse and rider capable of gaining good marks in this phase, are equally gifted when it comes to jumping across country and in the stadium. In England even the few remaining 'old school' scoffers have come to realize that despite the outlandish name, elementary dressage is, in essence the same schooling as that employed by the nagsman of old for 'making' a young horse.

Another arguable point concerning the dressage phase is the influence it does, or should exert on the outcome of the competition as a whole. This is now dealt with by a complicated and varying system of scoring that, in theory, ensures the relative influence exerted by the dressage to be slightly more than that of the show jumping, but considerably less than that of the cross-country.

The second phase of a combined training competition concerns endurance, and the ability to gallop and jump across country within a tight time limit. As a species, horses are outstanding athletes, although this ability obviously varies according to breed and type, and from horse to horse as much as it does with human athletes. To a greater or lesser degree horses also possess a keen spirit of competition and that indefinable characteristic called 'heart'. These are the physical and mental qualities that man utilizes in many different ways to combine with his own competitive instincts, and without which few equestrian sports could exist. But also like man, a horse has to be skilfully taught to bring out its best, learns by experience, and has to be conditioned physically and mentally over a period of time gauged according to the level at which it is required to compete.

Even the pony entered for a Pony Club Horse Trial has to be schooled and made fit to a degree. No horse can be entered for a one-day trial to find out what it is about, and then turned into a three-day eventer within a matter of a week or two, and even if it were possible there are stringent rules for qualifying that ensure such a thing could not occur. For a three-day event that on the second day includes many miles of roads and tracks and a steeplechase in addition to the ardours of the cross-country course, the physical conditioning of the horse does not fall very far short of that necessary for competing in long distance or endurance riding.

Much of the success or failure in the third phase of an event, the show jumping section, is also dependent on the fitness of the horse. The jumps are of no great height or spread, but the course, while presenting no problems to the show jumping fraternity as such, is designed to test the capabilities of a horse, passed fit to continue on the morning of that third day, but inevitably tired and stiff to a degree after the exertions of the previous day.

One of the fascinations of combined training is that it is a long term policy. There are no real short cuts even for the one-day eventer, and for the ambitious it is a long-drawn-out, time-consuming sport that is entirely absorbing. To combine the requirements of three different types of equitation in one horse and one rider, calls for dedication as the first quality of those who wish to event, at whatever level. But here is a sport where you can use the lower stratas as stepping stones to higher things, or as an end in themselves. Either way, combined training is one of the most satisfying, demanding, and challenging sports in the world.

In Britain combined training, unlike most sports, has developed from the top down. It began with the Olympics, then continued with the Three-Day Horse Trials at Badminton before spreading out at the lower levels to the one-day competitions that are the life blood of this form of equestrianism. Nowadays the majority of British event riders, and many of those in the United States and Australia, acquire their taste for the sport on the bottom rung of all, as members of the Pony Club.

When that admirable institution was formed in 1930, inter-branch competing of any kind was not encouraged, let alone any concerning a pastime that was then virtually unknown outside the Continent. Today the original excellent Pony Club objectives remain. The members are still aided to ride and enjoy all forms of equestrian sport; they are instructed in horsemanship and the care of their animals, and the Club does its best to inspire the ideals of true sportsmanship that cultivate strength of character. These are still the official aims of what is now a recognized youth organization with around 50,000 members and associates in the United Kingdom alone, but since the Second World War the competitive age in which we live has also been acknowledged. In addition to its normal activities, the Pony Club now provides an exciting range of inter-branch competitions, designed to cope with the varying abilities and ambitions of its more competitive minded members and to provide the first stepping stones towards the world of adult competing.

Initially at area qualifying rounds, then at championship level, branches can enter a team to do battle in the mounted games for the Prince Philip Cup for show jumping, or the Pony Club Polo Tournament for the boys only, the very popular tetrathlon; and for eventing which originated in 1949 and was the first Pony Club inter-branch competition to be organized.

Richard Meade, one of the most famous names in eventing, winner of three Olympic gold medals and, with Jane Bullen, the first product of the Pony Club to make Olympic level, joined the Club when he was five, and nine years later began his eventing career with the Monmouth branch. With a family background of horses and hunting, a little youthful experience of the show ring and marked success in the rough and tumble of gymkhana races, Richard and his 13.2 h.h. pony, Sandy, were chosen for the Monmouth team making their début at the qualifying area Pony Club Horse Trials, only a few years after inter-branch eventing got under way. For Richard this initiation was not an unqualified success as he was eliminated at the last jump on the cross-country, a large water-trough to which Sandy took exception, but the experience inspired him with an abiding interest in this new sport.

In the following summer of 1954 the Monmouth branch decided to have another go at the Horse Trials Championships, and a good neighbour, the famous show jumping expert, Colonel Llewellyn, loaned the team his Grade C jumper, St Teilo. Richard, by then fifteen and in search of a larger mount with more jumping ability, was given the ride, and during those summer holidays in the weeks before the area competition, spent hours each day at the Colonel's home getting to grips with the horse. Luck was with him. His mentor, Harry Llewellyn's German groom, was a brilliant instructor and just the man to develop Richard's undoubted ability. He was also well qualified to instil the principles of basic dressage, an essential too often lacking for many years from most British tuition.

In the event hard work and inspired teaching paid off. The Monmouth team won the area trials and went through to the Championships at Tetbury, in Gloucestershire, to come second in the team competition, with Richard also winning the individual Boys' Championship. After that moment of glory it was to be some years before even a vague dream of three-day eventing could materialize, but it was with the Pony Club that Richard Meade's appetite was created for the sport at which he continues to excel.

Richard Walker, partnered by Pasha, the same little Anglo-Arab with which he came up from Pony Club competitions to win the individual Junior European Championships in 1968, won the Badminton Horse Trials in the following year. At eighteen, the lowest age permissible, he is still the youngest rider to have achieved this feat, which he crowned later in the same season when included in the British team, winners that year of the adult European Championships at Haras du Pin.

Like the majority of women riders at the top of the eventing tree, Janet Hodgson, the battered, courageous heroine of the European Championships at Kiev in 1973, began on the eventing trail that led her there by competing at Pony Club level, in her case with the South Staffordshire branch. Mary Gordon-Watson, Olympic rider, World and European Champion is another Pony Club product. So too is Debbie West, with her intrepid little Baccarat one of the most consistently placed 'veterans' of three-day eventing, and second to Princess Anne in the European Championships at Burghley in 1971. But the biggest feather in the Pony Club cap to date, is the proud fact that the British team that brought the gold home from the Munich Olympics in 1972, were all ex-Pony Club members.

Since combined training was originally the exclusive province of the military, it is not surprising that, despite mechanization of the cavalry the tradition persists and the army continues to produce keen and successful event riders. Captain Mark Phillips, First The Queen's Dragoon Guards, who married Princess Anne in 1973, Olympic gold medallist, triple winner at Badminton and a victor at Burghley, is one of the best riders in combined training in the world. It was with the Beaufort branch of the Pony Club, where Mark was quickly recognized as outstanding, that his natural bent was encouraged and expanded. He rode in the team five years in succession, the first time when he was about twelve and riding a 14.2 h.h. pony. That year the Championships were at Wells and Mark was in the good company of Jane Bullen, Mike Tucker and George Weldon, son of Lieutenant-Colonel Weldon, their instructor (who with his great horse Kilbarry had dominated much of the eventing scene in the fifties).

The army is not the only one of the services to produce addicts of combined training. The life of a naval officer does not exactly lend itself to the time necessary for training rider and horse, but in 1955 Lieutenant-Commander Oram was in the British team that won the European Championships. And the fact that life in a nuclear submarine makes an event rider's aspirations even more difficult to fulfil, does not dampen the enthusiasm of Lieutenant-Commander Edwin Atkinson, who competes in three-day events whenever leave makes it possible, and who first caught the 'bug' as a successful member of the East Kent Pony Club team.

Princess Anne, individual champion in the 1971 European Champion-ships and included in the Olympic team at Montreal in 1976, did not really begin eventing until she was seventeen. But if, as according to her, she was too old before she knew anything about the sport, she was another who did acquire at least a flavour at Pony Club and similar level. She joined the Garth branch of the Pony Club in 1962 and attended rallies and rode in several of their competitions. Her first ever 'official' horse trial was a small affair organized at novice standard by the same branch. But Anne shares the royal family's liking for speed, and batting round a junior hunter trial course, in the early days with Bandit, the game little Welsh pony she shared with

Prince Charles, was considerably more to her taste than anything as slow as dressage. Like the majority of children at that age, this training on the ground appeared to be a boring exercise comprizing certain movements that had to be learned in order to take part in a horse trial. Jumping and galloping were fun, the things that mattered, and to an extent remained so for some while after the Princess went to boarding school, when for most terms she kept her good pony, High Jinks, at the nearby Moat House Riding Establishment.

Fortunately this riding school was run by Mrs Hatton-Hall, one-time show jumper and eventer, and an exponent of the art and advantages of dressage. This form of tuition was of such obvious benefit to both rider and pony, that gradually basic dressage began to make sense, and Anne's successes in the Moat House inter-school competitions began to grow. Before she left school to embark on fresh fields with Alison Oliver, the idea of eventing seriously at adult level was much more than a vague thought.

Whether those riders that make the top grade begin their eventing at Pony Club age, or plunge straight in at adult novice level, as children most of them appear to share some of the same mental and physical attributes that, broadly speaking, make up the two main categories of successful riders. There are the Mark Phillipses of this world, born to a background which includes horses and ponies as a matter of course and apparently also with the innate ability to ride. Mark started very young with an old, wise pony called Beauty. At six years old, he took on Pickles, a strong, horse-like pony of the same age with which he battled for the next two or three years, and although there were inevitable moments when he was frightened, there was never the remotest idea of 'not wanting to ride'. By the time Mark was nine, physically stronger himself and considerably more versed in the wiles of his pony, he had turned a notoriously unsuccessful partnership into a very happy and fortunate one.

Children like this never seem to go through the nervous phases suffered by so many, and however tough the going, their relationships with their ponies seem to be made up of all the fun and few of the anxieties that from time to time beset the less blessed. Maybe Lucinda Prior-Palmer, winner at Badminton, European champion in 1973, and included in the team sent to represent this country at Montreal, is correct in thinking that luck plays a big part in the making of a future three-day event rider. A child or young teenager, however keen, has only to have a really bad fall, or injure a pony, or have it off work for a long time through lameness, to lose heart and interest, if not in riding at least in the competitive side.

The other type of riders who make great horsemen are those without the

4

fearlessness that goes with innate ability, who learn to master their 'nerves' and too vivid imaginations, and make the top through sheer determination. Sometimes these are riders who, like Richard Meade, make the grade by the application of intellect to the problems and challenges involved. But whether horsemanship is inborn or acquired, there are few if any top-class eventers who were more than momentarily frightened of horse or pony as a child. Combined training is too tough and demanding a sport for the basically nervous rider.

They may well have had their moments. Richard, taken hunting at the age of seven, was let off the leading rein by a groom with more optimism than sense, and the pony promptly carried its small rider through a thicket of painfully scratchy brambles en route for hounds. Richard was scared as well as hurt, but even at that age there was no break in his determination to ride.

Obviously the parents' attitude plays a big part in the children's outlook towards riding and hazards in general, and in encouraging the right mental approach in would-be top-class horsemen and competitors. As a child Lucinda's relaxed and happy outlook towards competing was an echo of her parents' good sense about the subject, an attitude shared by most whose children have made it to the top. It was fun to enter for this and that, the gymkhana games at a local show, a try at junior hunter trials, and given the luck, a win or a place was a bonus to the overall enjoyment of the day, the rosette a prized memento. But the outcome of the competition was almost incidental. Jupiter was a much loved New Forest pony with a mind of his own. He partnered Lucinda in a great many Pony Club dos of every kind, but since nothing on earth would make him jump higher than 2 feet 6 inches, and he was adept at taking off with his front legs and bringing them down in exactly the same spot, they seldom won anything. That didn't matter at all, the enjoyment lay in the mutual confidence and companionship of a pony, in having the chance to compete, to have the opportunity of being there at all. This outlook has nothing to do with the will to win essential in the make-up of any competitor, at whatever the age, whatever the grade, whatever the sport, and certainly demonstrated by Lucinda Prior-Palmer and her success in the international field. But it has a lot to do with the fact that whether she won or lost, her competing in childhood was totally lacking in the stress and tensions too often surrounding the child competitor with ambitious parents, and that she learned to know competing as a sport.

A well-known horseman is not alone in thinking that despite the world explosion of interest in horses and ponies, in riding and driving and the competitive sports that go with them, the overall standard of horsemanship in Britain is not improving and is, in fact, lower than it used to be. There could be various reasons for this, not least the modern lack of a horse-minded background in the majority of families, but he thinks it could also be that too many children are taught too much, too young.

Dressage, as such, was late in being accepted in England. Then it was realized that, correctly understood and applied, it is the key to horses and ponies that are a joy to ride and more successful in competing, and the training has been taken up in a big way – but not always by those experienced in the art or qualified to teach it. Although there are always a few exceptions, children under ten or eleven cannot be expected to have any real understanding of dressage, nor is it desirable that they should be given dressage instruction. They are not capable of such niceties as putting their ponies on the bit or of 'educating' them, and unqualified tuition that is often too advanced for the rider's mental age and physical abilities with too much emphasis on correct aids and exact position of legs and seat, can result in stiff, over-anxious little riders who lose much of the balance that is the heritage of childhood.

Young children, left to themselves, do ride principally by the natural balance that is an essential ingredient of good horsemanship. Given a quiet pony and sufficient instruction to ensure that the rider is safe and leaves the pony's mouth alone, the emphasis at those stages should then be on fun, playing Red Indians, and establishing a happy relationship between mount and rider.

Much of Princess Anne's eventing success is due to the happy mutual confidence she enjoys with her horses, and that stems from the uncomplicated fun she had riding as a child. Anne has inherited the Queen's rapport with horses and ponies, and gleaned the first rudiments of riding and a fund of 'horse-sense' from the same source. But otherwise, apart from what she learned from the family groom who helped with the children's riding activities, there was little formal instruction until she and Charles were given the occasional short series of lessons by Miss Sybil Smith, the well-known and experienced instructor of the young.

Anne was twelve when she and Charles joined the Garth Pony Club, and that involved attending some of the instructional working rallies. Otherwise, until she was thirteen and went to boarding school, her equestrian activities took place mostly in the relaxed atmosphere of her homes, where she and her pony enjoyed themselves charging around the grounds and exploring their increasing potential.

By the summer holidays of 1962 Anne's pony partner was High Jinks, an

Irish bred, sensible all-rounder of 14.2 h.h., with a good temperament and natural ability, but in no way either a 'blood' type or the expensive kind of creature sometimes seen at the Pony Club Championships. Still in the royal mews at Windsor and used for fun riding, the pony was only five when he arrived, and although well-schooled his experience of competing just about equalled that of his new rider. He proved to be mistrustful of ditches, a phobia that had to be overcome, but was otherwise always co-operative about jumping the variety of small fences that made up a miniature cross-country course around the Home Park at Windsor, or any other reasonable obstacles that came his way. After a period of getting to know each other Anne and Jinks embarked on their first encouraging ventures into Junior Pony Club Hunter Trials and novice jumping. They shared the same liking for galloping and jumping across country, and as the standard grew higher the successes kept pace. Despite the 'bore' of the dressage phase, Anne was beginning to take an interest in novice Pony Club Horse Trials as worthwhile fields to conquer. In Jinks the Princess had exactly the right type of ordinary pony with a good temperament, that jumped freely and with the right schooling would give any keen young rider an enjoyable and, with a modicum of luck, successful entry into the world of Pony Club eventing.

Although ponies are increasingly popular with younger children in Australia and America, in those countries, unlike England, they have never been the traditional mounts of the young. In the junior division of American Pony Club Horse Trials there may be a number of ponies, but no more than five per cent in the Regional Rallies – the equivalent of our Area Trials – and the percentage drops sharply as the competitions get stiffer. When it comes to the American Pony Club Championships, except for the occasional brilliant pony, horses are the order of the day.

When the Pony Club was first founded in Britain its title was an exact description of what it was. In those days all children, even the older ones rode ponies, and when the competing side of the Club was introduced competitions and courses were automatically geared to the smaller animal. This remains true of the Mounted Games and show jumping competitions, but more horses than ponies are now competing at the horse trial championships. The young of today do tend to be taller and heavier than previous generations, and when it comes to Pony Club associates aged seventeen to twenty, they are in effect adults and the horses they ride may well be those with which they continue their eventing careers.

Some of the horses competing at this level are ridden also in adult events. There is no height limit, and the restrictions concern only horses graded as advanced (Grade 1) in the current, or two previous years of the British Horse Society's register of combined training, or those placed first or second in an official BHS Intermediate or Advanced Horse Trial during the same period of time. Otherwise any event horse can compete at Pony Club level so long as it is not under five years old, has not been ridden more than once in the same year in PC Area Trials or Championships, and in order to qualify has been regularly ridden at rallies by a Pony Club member.

There is talk of bringing in a rule further to restrict event horses that also compete in adult BHS competitions, and also to lower the age limit of associates, and it might well be sensible and more in keeping with Pony Club objectives to implement both ideas.

When it comes to the Championships some pony owning members tend to think they stand little chance of being selected for a team in what appears to be an increasingly horse orientated world, but there is nothing about the type of cross-country course built for these occasions that is beyond the scope of a well-schooled 14 h.h. pony, give or take an inch or two. The horses may, or may not, have the edge in galloping and therefore in the time factor, but the length is only $1-1\frac{1}{4}$ miles at area trials and $\frac{1}{4}$ mile longer at the Championships, and that is no more difficult for a fit pony than for a horse. There are not less than twelve obstacles, not more than sixteen, on an area cross-country, not more than twenty at the Championships, with a maximum height of 3 feet 6 inches, maximum spread of 7 feet. The show jumps are 3 inches higher. And if the distances between combinations are constructed with maybe a horse's stride in mind, ponies, adept at finding a fifth leg where necessary, are often better ·equipped for coping with situations where the longer striding horse finds itself in difficulties. For the ambitious without the means or maybe inclination to keep a horse, the answer lies with schooling and fitness far more than with size or type of animal.

The Pony Club Horse Trials organized by the various branches are always geared to ponies, and the annual open affairs usually have a lower standard yet, many including a junior novice competition as well. This is where beginners can start to find out what the sport entails, but since a great deal of time, work and trouble is involved in organizing even a Pony Club Horse Trial, it is not always easy to find sufficient competitions suited to the complete novice rider and, or, pony. Hunting and junior hunter trials both provide excellent experience in going across country and jumping fixed fences, and the majority of gymkhanas include a class where the novice can put into practice the show jumping skills learned with a few coloured fences at home. Practice in a dressage test, as such, is not easy to come by outside a horse trial, but whether it is necessary depends on the individual's definition of the art. There are those who consider dressage starts at Prix St George standard; others rightly think the first steps in dressage are when the young horse or pony ceases to play up, and carries its rider better each day than the one before.

Primarily dressage is a progressive system for training a horse with a rider on its back to be in balance, to go forward with an even rhythm, to be supple and immediately obedient to light leg, seat, and hand aids. According to outlook that is either 'basic training' or 'elementary dressage', but either way the dressage test is not the end product. The test, at whatever standard, is a check-up, a method of discovering whether the idea is working out right. At top dressage level the aim is to produce a horse that can be handed to any good rider who fully understands the correct aids, and it will then co-operate with him, in any way he asks, as easily and pleasantly as though he had been riding it for years. If the horse will only perform these movements, no matter how advanced, within the confines of a dressage arena, then the message has been misinterpreted.

The movements required in the Pony Club Championship dressage tests are not demanding. No collection is asked for, and a fluent test with the pony supple, obedient and calm is likely to be better marked than greater accuracy with a wooden-headed animal. At the lower standards obviously less is expected of the competitors.

A pony that accepts the bit, holding it lightly in its mouth with a relaxed jaw; that is active, particularly in the hind-quarters; and obedient in all ways, from standing still to be mounted to going forward freely with the slightest leg pressure, is likely to be as successful in the dressage test as it is a joy to ride across country. But it is an aim that takes time to achieve, and even the best trained pony cannot be expected to perform well without some conditioning and schooling for some time beforehand. If it is a young animal with little experience, then its training just cannot be hurried.

A corner of a paddock, marked out or roped off to roughly the size of the dressage arena used for Pony Club tests, should be about 20 by 40 metres (66 by 132 feet), with the appropriate marker letters painted on old oil cans. A confined space is always an asset in schooling and gives rider and pony the 'feel' of working in an area of the required size, but most of the training can be, and should be a part of the daily ride.

Millcroft Aries, a 13.1 h.h. Welsh pony, famous throughout Devon for his victories in seven different fields of competing, ridden by a light-weight adult, includes Riding Club eventing amongst his activities. He was hacked as a four-year-old, and then schooled almost entirely on the road, first at walk and slow trot, then building up to include as much hill work as possible to engage his hocks and muscle him up. As time passed the pony's basic training progressed through half-halts and shoulder-ins to leg yielding and half-passes, all learned and performed while out riding the quiet Devon lanes. By eight years old Aries was schooled to elementary standard in dressage. He has competed and won at Pony Club standard, and in the six, mostly open riding club events he was entered for in 1975, he won three, came second twice, and was fifth at the other, taking on horses of all sizes and types. His dressage marks for each movement averaged out at sevens or eights, and at one competition where the judges were marking very low, Aries' total of 52 dressage penalties was still 20 better than the next highest. Aries won the supreme championship of the Welsh Performance Competition, organized by the Welsh Pony and Cob Society, in both 1974 and 1975 and was also champion Combined Training Pony. In 1976 he competed in the East Cornwall Riding Club Two-Day Event. His dressage score was 18 penalty points, and he was a minute within the time over $5\frac{1}{2}$ miles of roads and tracks. He was unpenalized over the steeplechase of 1 mile with six fences, and the same over an eighteen-fence cross-country course, all at approximately 3 feet and including a trakener, a Normandy bank, a coffin, and a 6 feet wide, 3 feet deep 'chasm'. Because of his size Aries had to gallop all the way to achieve the time, but he went clear in the show-jumping and won the competition. As the judge wrote on Aries' dressage sheet, 'What a fantastic pony!' Obviously this is a pony that has been schooled above average, but a lot of his success, be it in show jumping, show pony and working pony classes, at Prix Caprilli contests, dressage and jumping, hunter trials and eventing, are due to the tremendous zest he brings to every type of competition. This is partly owing to the fact that he has never been bored, and that his schooling is incorporated into the daily ride.

Schooling a horse or pony must always be a flexible business because each animal has to be considered and treated as an individual, and much of the prejudice against dressage arose through the sheer boredom experienced by horses and riders alike who confined their training to going round and round an arena or indoor school. Wherever the schooling takes place an imaginative rider can devise fresh ways for keeping mutual interest, but everything that goes into a dressage test is the demonstration of what makes a horse or pony a more pleasant animal to ride out, and that is where most of its training should take place.

It is easy enough, and adds interest to a ride, to practise controlling the pony's back end, and so help in positioning its head, to try for rhythm in all the paces, and for instant obedience, just as the best practice for jumping is to get in the way of popping over any suitable little obstacle, from a twig to a hurdle, including ditches and water whenever possible. There are endless variations to just riding straight ahead, such as always attempting smooth transitions when changing pace and speed, combining half-halts, an aid to suppling, with trotting and cantering, and asking the pony to rein-back correctly when halted, or to do a turn on the forehand. There are tracks where serpentines can be practised, open spaces in which to ride circles, bends and corners to utilize in getting a few paces at the shoulder-in. So long as the training consists of first getting the pony relaxed and obedient and then working up gradually to the various movements required in basic dressage, the end product should be an animal that is a pleasure to ride whatever the job in hand – and not just a passable performer between the four white boards of a dressage arena.

The dressage test used in the Pony Club Championships is always one officially devised by the British Horse Society. It has to be memorized by the rider and the time to learn it is before attempting any of the movements with the pony. Some people like to learn it by using paper and pencil, but one of the most foolproof methods is to mark an arena in miniature on the lawn, and do the whole thing over on one's own two feet until it is unforgettable. Once mounted, the rider can then concentrate on the pony responding correctly, without thought for what comes next. In fact the actual test should be practised very seldom or the pony will start anticipating, and all the movements are best rehearsed out of sequence.

The number of riders who can be chosen to represent their branch at the Area Horse Trials, from which the winners go on to the Championships, is obviously limited, but the more trouble taken over training horse or pony, the more likelihood there is of being selected. Those who are asked to train for the inter-branch team competition or for the senior individual competition, open to associate members eighteen years of age or over, normally receive special instruction – but it is up to the rider to see that the animal is fit.

At the lowest levels of Pony Club eventing a pony that lives out, so long as it is not grossly fat and has been given adequate concentrates and exercise, should have no difficulty in coping with the not very arduous demands of such a horse trial – and given the opportunity would probably do two a week quite happily. Competing at the standard of present day area and championship competitions is another matter, and grass-fed ponies cannot be expected to produce the speed or stamina required. Ponies do benefit both physically and mentally from an hour or so of grazing out of the twenty-four, but otherwise, if the animal is to be given the chance of proving its real worth when chosen for the team, and being physically capable of completing the competition, it should be stabled for some weeks beforehand, and then fed, groomed, exercised, and treated accordingly.

So much for one way of entry into the world of combined training, and there are young riders who, however keen, for one reason and another can go no further than the ultimate in Pony Club Horse Trials. Others, lucky enough to have the means, time, dedication, horse and ability, set their sights on the very different, and very tough world of adult three-day eventing. Some of these arrive at their objective via, in the first instance, the benefit of the training scheme connected to the Junior European Three-Day Event Championship, devised to bridge the yawning gap between Pony Club Horse Trials and combined training at the top.

The idea stems from 1965, when the Duke of Edinburgh became President of the FEI (Fédération Equestre Internationale), and put forward a suggestion for a training scheme plus international three-day events for young riders under twenty-one. Oddly enough the arguments against such a plan were many, ranging from the big fences being too large for competitors mounted on ponies, as many still were in those days, to riders at the younger end of the age group, the fourteen-year-old, finding the mental problems connected with international three-day eventing too much of a strain. Eventually however the Junior Three-Day Event Committee was formed under Colonel Moseley, who remained the guiding force until his retirement and subsequent death in 1975, when Colonel Allfrey took over.

Once initiated, the original problems then included finding a method of choosing a team, interesting other nations in the project, and getting a suitable venue in Europe. By 1966 Italy had offered to hold the competition at the end of July, five other countries had agreed to take part, and the parents of about twenty young British riders who had acquitted themselves well in the previous year's Pony Club Championships, had been asked in confidence if their young could be considered for short-listing.

By then the upper age limit had been fixed at twenty, either horses or ponies could be ridden, and the event was to be run under CCI (Concours Complet International) rules with a few modifications. The final team selections were made after trials at Crookham and Tidworth, and by 20 July six excited young riders and their mounts were within a few days of setting off when travel and quarantine difficulties, arising from an attack of swamp fever in France, nullified the entire project.

In the following year it looked as though once again luck would not be with this new venture. A British team was already trained and picked for the competition to be held in conjunction with the adult Eridge Horse Trials, when for various reasons all the other countries withdrew except for France. The decision was taken to go ahead regardless, and the competition was arranged as a match between the two countries. As the French team consisted of three boys, the British riders were divided into two teams, one of boys and one of girls, and both, to their surprise, were beaten by the invaders. But the competition proved so enjoyable and successful that when it was staged in France a year later five nations entered teams.

The top age limit was then lowered to eighteen and the host nation was allowed to enter up to eight individuals, four of which rode in the team. The worth of the Junior European Three-Day Event was made evident in 1969 when Richard Walker, the previous year's winner, took on the world's best at Badminton Horse Trials and beat them. Since then the names of other young riders, and of horses, who triumphed in the junior competition, are now known throughout the eventing world. British riders and horses include Angela Martin-Bird, Pamela and Amanda Sivewright, Aly Pattinson, the Olympic horse, Our Nobby, then ridden by Jane Bullen's sister, Jennie, and Tony Hill with his Maid Marion, one of Mark Phillips's 'chance rides' with which he won Burghley 1973. Lucinda Prior-Palmer and Be Fair gained valuable experience as members of the British junior European team that won in 1971.

Virginia Holgate is another who came up to the top via the Junior Championships. She began her riding career as a small child perched on the backs of polo pony types in the Philippine Islands, and later was for a short while a member of the Singapore Pony Club. But competing did not come within her orbit, either then or when the family returned to England and Virginia, still at school, attended Moat House for weekly riding lessons. As far as she was concerned both dressage and three-day eventing were a closed book, she knew nothing of either and her joy in riding was principally 'just galloping at fences!' It was not until she left school that the obvious jumping potential of her little horse Dubonnet, then an inexperienced four-year-old, sent her seeking knowledgeable advice. What she and her mother then learned about combined training, and the help and encouragement Virginia and her horse received, fired her interest and set her on the eventing trail that was to lead to victory in the 1975 mini-Olympics in Montreal. But before that there was a long way to go.

She started competing when Dubonnet was five, with a few hunter trials and a Pony Club Area Horse Trial. Then came five one-day events under BHS rules, and the success and optimism produced by their results tempted them to have a go at Tidworth, the three-day event staged especially for 'first timers'. To Virginia's inexperienced eyes the cross-country appeared horrific, the steeplechase equally impossible, the roads and tracks a maze where she would inevitably get lost and could see no way of working out the timing. It may have been nerve-wracking, and the reaction of a rider singularly free from 'nerves' is a pointer to the gulf between one-day trials and three-day events, but the performance Virginia and Dubonnet put up that day combined with their previous record to bring them to the junior team selector's notice.

In 1972 she and Dubonnet were asked to compete as an individual entry in the Junior Championships at Eridge. Good dressage marks, a clear on the steeplechase course and a wonderful gallop across country until there were only three fences to go, were marred when too fast an approach and a slippery exit up a bank landed Dubonnet on his side. The mistake cost them the usual 60 penalty points and they finished twenty-fourth on the day, but that made no difference to the pair's evident ability. A year later they were included in the junior team and set off for the Championships being held at Pompadour, one of the French State Studs.

The event was very well organized and the setting beautiful. The dressage arena, where the test was ridden on sand, was sited in front of the magnificent house. Luck was with Virginia during the roads and tracks phase, from which the tracks had been omitted, when an amused French family pointed out that she and Dubonnet were gaily trotting off to Paris, having failed to notice a direction flag pointing in the opposite direction. The steeplechase, laid out on the race-course, gave a wonderful ride despite the going alternating slow sand with faster turf which presented a slight problem with timing, and a variety of fences strange to English eyes. There were sloping white railings over the water ditch, stone walls to negotiate, and even the more normal 'chase fences looked unfamiliar, constructed with laurel in place of brush or birch, which many horses either wasted time in jumping instead of brushing through the top or occasionally attempted to bank.

The cleverly planned cross-country course was laid out over exacting, very hilly terrain. It was designed so that the big fences came at the top or bottom of the hills and along the flat they were posts and rails. One moment the horses were coming up or descending to a formidable bullfinch or table fence, the next they were pushing on over a 3 feet upright. It was a big course and the weather was unbearably sultry, but the British horses were fit and acquitted themselves with honour. The Irish bred horses which the Italians were riding were, like those of the Irish team, also fit, and in the final placings these teams came second and third respectively, but for many it was a sad and sorry tale. The majority of the continental horses were in no physical shape to be asked to tackle such a course. The falls and refusals were legion, and in a number of ugly instances exhausted animals came to a stop and, literally incapable of moving, had to be pushed out of the way – a disgraceful, if salutary illustration of the supreme importance of getting a three-day event horse fit for the job in hand.

The fences in the show jumping phase were low, but required jumping with care because the majority were built with wide spreads. It was also unusual to find a course that led out of the arena over a fence, round a large bush and then with a jump back in again.

The final results at Pompadour were a triumph for the British juniors who made it a team victory for the third year running, while Virginia Holgate and Dubonnet triumphed to become the individual European junior champions. However, in the following year Britain's team was vanquished in Rome, more by an almost impossible cross-country course than lack of ability, but in 1975, when the Junior Championships were held at Cirencester Park, the spoils came home once more, with the British team taking both team and individual gold medals, and seven of the ten first places.

Prince Philip's original scheme for aiding the young event rider is now of such repute and popularity that the selectors are almost overwhelmed with applications to compete in the initial stages. These are special classes held at chosen one-day horse trials, from which the results provide a short list to go forward for a final trial and further training before a team is chosen. But although the lowest age limit for riders remains at fourteen and the no-height limit for horses is retained, the standard of the competition is now so high, with fences built to correspond, that even to be considered for short list selection a younger rider, or a pony, would have to be of outstanding brilliance, the pony comparable to C. Brooke's famous little Olive Oyl with which he became individual junior champion in 1971.

As the rules now stand, all horses must be at least six years old, and must never have competed in a CCIO (Concours Complet International Officiel), Olympic or Regional Games. With the exception of the host nation, which may field an extra two individual riders, each country may enter up to six competitors. From these a final team of four is selected, the three best scores to count, and the remaining two riders compete as individuals. All competitors, whether riding as team members or not, have an equal chance of winning the individual Championship. Junior three-day events count in qualifying horses and riders for competing in the adult equivalents.

Each grade of combined training demands different degrees of schooling and courage from the horse, and competent, all-round horsemanship from its rider; this is the challenge that makes the sport so popular throughout many different standards of horsemanship.

The official BHS One-Day Horse Trials are very unlike three-day events in the demands they make on horse and rider, but are basically a modified version of the same competition. Normally divided into novice, intermediate or open sections, sometimes with the last two combined, or omitting one or another of the grades, these competitions provide the more ambitious with the essential means of training for more arduous three-day events. Like all riders at the top, Princess Anne and Mark Phillips bring on their young horses by riding in the appropriate grades of one-day trials, and each season refresh the old hands by riding in a few trials comprising the requisite class. But although they both use the trials as part of their training schedule their outlook on these competitions is not quite the same. In a one-day event Anne does not really set out to prove anything very much except that the horse is feeling well, jumping capably, and doing everything to her satisfaction. Mark has more of the competitive outlook, riding each competition as a competition, but at the same time there are days when winning is not specifically the objective. On these occasions the trial is used as a warm-up for a more important event in the future, and although Mark, like anyone else is always happy to win, what he would have in mind would be achieving some particular purpose with his horse on that day. Sometimes the lesser three-day or two-day events are used in the same way by both riders. In those trials they enter as a preliminary to a major competition like Badminton, both are pleased if victory comes their way, but like all those with a planned programme the object is to give the horses a good trip, and for the sake of a first place it would be mad to go batting round a cross-country and risk bringing them, already exhausted, to face the rigours to come. Chance injury during everyday training is quite common enough with horses of this calibre to take any unwarranted chances, as the Princess ruefully appreciated in March 1976. With Goodwill excused Badminton as an Olympic possible, one day Anne was happily training both Flame

Gun and Arthur of Troy, her two second-strings, for the event, and in less than a week both were sufficiently lame to be out of it, leaving their owner without a ride.

For the majority of combined training riders who, from inclination or lack of the means have no thought of going further up the scale, one-day horse trials are an end in themselves. And for those who cannot take on this type of official BHS trial, the Riding Clubs' competitions offer a satisfying alternative.

In Britain the official Riding Clubs movement for riders over seventeen is administered by the British Horse Society, and has its headquarters at the National Equestrian Centre at Kenilworth, in Warwickshire. It is an active and forward looking association, its declared objective: 'To assist and encourage those interested in the horse and equitation, to improve and maintain the standard of riding and horsemanship, and to seek to preserve and develop public riding facilities.' For club purposes the country is divided into regions, each supporting a number of clubs, and these provide a wide and satisfying range of activities, both equestrian and social, to suit all tastes.

The competitions include one-day eventing, the standard ranging from the inter-club trials that are within the scope of quite moderate horses and riders, to that of the Riding Clubs' Horse Trials Championships, an official event organized or sponsored by the BHS, and held annually at the Equestrian Centre. For this the club teams first compete at area trials, the winners then going forward to contest the championship.

With some exceptions this top competition is run under normal BHS rules for combined training, but the length of the cross-country and show jumping courses, the height and spread of obstacles and the minimum time allowed, are all fixed at a slightly lower standard than that used in the novice section of official BHS One-Day Horse Trials, enabling a different stamp of horse and rider to compete.

Most good horses start their eventing careers in Riding Club competitions, but the rules for the official area trials and the championships, exclude: any horse under five years old, any that has won £15 or more in official BHS trials (a horse that has won £6 or more is penalized with 20 penalty points), those that have taken part in any BHS trial over the same course as the Riding Clubs' championships. And any rider who has ridden the same course in a BHS trial is also ineligible.

There is no height limit for any but the area and championship competitions, and for those it is now a rule that all horses must exceed 14 h.h. Sadly this now eliminates the brilliant little ponies such as Aries from top

Riding Club competing, but it does cater for the rider with a good all-round 14.2 h.h. pony, now out of Pony Club and longing to continue competing with the same animal, but ineligible for official BHS trials where the height limit is 15 h.h. And in this day of ever-rising costs it is a big consideration to be able to continue satisfying one's competitive instinct with an animal that eats less, and is altogether a less expensive proposition than a horse.

There is one other category of eventing, designed for those who appreciate the virtues of that most versatile of breeds, the Arabian. Gone are the days when, absurdly, in England Arab horses were treated as beautiful baubles, fit for little else than showing in hand. Their endurance has never been in question, but now it is acknowledged that these horses jump well, and when properly schooled make no bones about water which is not part of their heritage. The size of the fences is governed to a degree by the relatively small size of the majority of the breed, but in dressage tests their brilliant, fluid movement is seen to advantage. Anglo-Arabs, that often combine the best of both worlds, have their roll of honour in international three-day eventing. Now the Arabian is catered for with two or three one-day trials held annually for pure and part bred horses, and the breed is proving once again that there are very few facets of the equestrian world for which it cannot be used.

2

Out of all riders who now make combined training their particular sport only a relatively small percentage make the grade to three-day events let alone the international teams and the pinnacle of the Olympics. Opportunity and means confine the majority to the one-day trials, but equally, although all forms of the sport call for some common qualities in the people involved, the successful three-day event rider has to have these in excess, besides certain extra attributes.

Nerve is an obvious necessity, as the years pass and the standard of the big competitions rises and the fences get more formidable, but with it must go natural ability and, most important of all, a real understanding of the horse. The rider at the top of three-day eventing is one who can ride the horse as it is going on that particular day. A horse is as much subject to 'off' days as a person, and it is because the Richard Meades and Mark Phillipses of this world can, almost unconsciously gauge, understand, and act on this fact, that they remain in the topmost ranks. If the horse is not going well in a training competition these top names ride it accordingly, but when the big day comes along their horses are ready, trained and fit to a hair for what has always been the real objective.

There is another quality essential for all with the ambition to get to the top – the grit, mental ability and consuming interest to start again from the bottom. However outstanding the horse, top grade three-day eventing makes big demands on its physique, three seasons at the top is quite a long while in the competitive life of an international eventer, and there are many full of initial promise that fall by the way before they make it at all.

When Britain won the gold medal for the Olympic Three-Day Event in Mexico in 1968, the team was captained by Major Derek Allhusen with his famous horse, Lochinvar. The career of this veteran event rider began in the middle fifties when he was partnered by a highly-strung, courageous little mare called Laurien. Before the Second World War her owner had won a regimental point-to-point and tried his hand at a little show jumping. When the war ended he managed to acquire a captured ex-German army transport mare for the princely sum of £50, with which he competed successfully in jumping competitions and also rode in the Pentathlon at the 1948 Winter Olympics. When this mare, Laura, broke down later that year she was put to stud, and her first foal, born in 1950, was Laurien, sired by Davy Jones, the horse that so nearly won the Grand National in 1936.

Despite Laurien's youth and her rider's inexperience in the field of combined training, their initial successes in the relatively few one-day horse trials of those days upgraded Laurien to advanced classes in 1956. They came fourth at Harewood that season, in the three-day event eventually superceded by Burghley, and qualified for the following year's Badminton, where they fell. Selected as a British team member to contest the 1957 European Championships in Copenhagen, Major Allhusen helped to win the gold and came fifth in the individual table. In the years that followed this pair were placed second and fourth at Badminton, and second at Harewood, helped win the silver in the 1959 European Championships and gained the bronze individual medal, and on points were the British Horse Trials champions two years running. Their sights were set on the 1960 Olympics in Rome, when Laurien became ill. She was retired the next year, but was to make a further considerable contribution to the history of eventing with the birth of a colt, that, christened Laurieston, became one of the famous names in the sport.

In the meantime, Laurien's owner began again. The replacement, Lochinvar, was bought in Ireland as a four-year-old that turned out to be a year younger, and having, in true Irish fashion, been hard-hunted as a two-year-old, arrived resembling the proverbial 'hat-rack'. With a difficult mouth, the result of ham-handed riders catching him in the back teeth over Irish banks, and a weak back, the legacy of carrying too much weight too young, Lochinvar presented a few problems. Time, patience, and initial light work on the lunge ironed out the horse's troubles to a degree. By 1963 Derek Allhusen was once more testing the first rungs of the eventing ladder that, with this horse were to lead, via wins and placings in one- and three-day events, and the European Championships, first in Moscow in 1965, then in Punchestown in 1967, and as British Horse Trials champions on three occasions, to the summit of ambition, the Olympics.

As a left-over from Lochinvar's youth, the aids and restrictions implicit in dressage and show jumping were always resented to some degree – in the dressage arena his swishing tail was usually penalized as a sign of resistance – and these two phases remained the horse's Achilles' heel all through his distinguished career. But Lochinvar's sustained brilliance on the steeplechase and cross-country courses combined with his own and his rider's undaunted courage to keep them in the forefront of eventing for many seasons, and as the sheet-anchor of the British team until 1969.

Of all the triumphs, Mexico in 1968 obviously stood out, where the team won the Olympic gold and Derek Allhusen and his horse the individual silver, but it was also the watershed in Lochinvar's eventing life. He did compete again, and he and his owner were in the victorious British team in the 1969 European Championships, but he was permanently retired in 1971 with increasing foot trouble – to enjoy an uninterrupted rest, well earned by a horse that as a top-class eventer jumped more than eight hundred fences without giving his rider a fall, and had only two 'stops' in the cross-country phase of nineteen consecutive three-day events.

Major Allhusen's own eventing, but not riding, career, came to an end in 1970 when he broke a leg schooling a young horse. He continued his own contribution to the sport in 1972, by lending Laurieston to Richard Meade for Munich, and so ensured the double triumph of two gold medals for Britain.

In the team led by Major Allhusen in Mexico, were Ben Jones, Jane Bullen, the first British woman to ride in an Olympic three-day event, and Richard Meade.

Ben Jones, now Equitation Officer of the equine wing of the Royal Army Veterinary Corps training centre at Melton Mowbray, then a Staff Sergeant of the King's Troop Royal Horse Artillery, had every opportunity to become a fine horseman, during years in a unit that is exclusively equestrian and prides itself on an excellent competing record. He first hit the top when he rode Master Bernard, a troop horse, in the 1964 Olympic team in Tokyo. For Mexico he was short-listed, with seven other riders, and partnered with Foxdor, the talented but not over-easy horse that Alison Oliver had been asked by the Combined Training Committee to prepare. Ben and the horse had been teamed up before, at Punchestown when Britain regained the European Championships after a lapse of three years, and they got on well together. The training was going according to plan when only a short while before flying out to Mexico City, Foxdor died from a heart attack. With such a task ahead there was little enough time for making a partnership with another animal, but Ben Jones took the ride on the loaned The Poacher, Martin Whiteley's great horse that was in every international team from 1966 to 1971, and under weather conditions that became notorious, helped materially to win the gold.

Maybe Jane Bullen could be said to be one of the exceptions that proves the rule. Since marriage she has evented other horses, but her somewhat meteoric ascent to the top concerned only one. She comes from a distinguished riding family, and after gleaning some of the art of riding across country in Pony Club Hunter Trials, started eventing, like her elder brothers and sisters, as a member of the Cattistock branch team. As one of Britain's top dressage riders, Jane's elder sister, now Jennie Loriston-Clarke, is a pointer to the fact that all the Bullen children assimilated the basics of dressage in the course of learning to ride, and this, combined with natural ability and a brave heart stood Jane in good stead when she took over the little family horse, Our Nobby. Though occasionally nappy, Nobby compensated for his lack of inches with great jumping ability and courage, and Jane's ventures at Pony Club level became increasingly successful. Even so it seemed over-ambitious in 1965, when she was still under age for qualifying her horse in adult competitions, to be setting her sights on Badminton 1966.

In fact the qualification difficulty was overcome by sister Jennie riding Our Nobby at Chatsworth in 1965, in the intermediate class, where they took third place, but owing to bad weather Badminton was cancelled in 1966 and Jane and her horse had to wait another year. In 1967, and to the surprise of many, they came fifth at Badminton and third at Burghley in the same season. Victory at Badminton in the spring of 1968 indisputably proved this pair's ability, and despite all the doubts at that time about girls riding in Olympic events, Jane and Our Nobby made it to Mexico, where their performance did much to dispel the prejudice.

Of the four members of that team Richard Meade was the one best qualified to prove that a top event rider has to be able to pick himself up when one horse meets with misfortune, and work back to the top with another. His first adult horse trial, the restricted novice class at a one-day affair in Northumberland, was in 1959 when he was twenty-one and riding his own mare, Embassy. Luck was with them and they won, but the mare had an impossible temperament and Richard was more than grateful when Colonel Llewellyn gave him an ex-race horse. Gazi gave his new owner the opportunity for gaining a lot more experience, and with it a lot of fun, and it was a very sad day when the horse broke its back out hunting with the drag hounds, and Richard was back to square one.

The loan of a good horse, Ad Astra, then brought a win at a big west of England Horse Trials, but a subsequent attempt at the newly organized three-day event at Burghley resulted in Ad Astra breaking down on the steeplechase course. The fates did not seem to be kindly disposed, but horse or no horse, Richard Meade was by then a dedicated would-be top-class three-day event rider. A look at the Rome Olympics as a spectator then left him with the inner conviction that, given a spot of luck and the right partner, he might well one day make the Olympics himself.

This ambition took a big step towards reality when he was given the permanent lease of a seven-year-old called Barberry, destined to be one of the future 'great horses' in combined training, although more than ordinarily accident prone. By breeding, conformation, natural talent and temperament, Barberry seemed cut out for the sport, and after a period of schooling followed by competing in novice trials, Richard and the horse were included in the team that won at an international students rally in Amsterdam.

The cross-country course had been moderately easy and after a third place in the Eridge Trials there was a win in the open class at Tweseldown, followed by another victory in the intermediate at Chatsworth. The interest the selectors were taking in the pair was intensified in the spring of 1963, when Richard and Barberry competed at Badminton and came second to Susan Fleet and The Gladiator. These good results earned them a place in the team in the unofficial three-day event at Munich that autumn, and it was encouraging to be placed fifteenth.

With his eyes on Tokyo, Richard was full of hope and determination for Badminton 1964, but to his chagrin the horse proved insufficiently fit and after blowing up in the steeplechase, had two stops and a fall across country.

Disappointed but undaunted Richard set about rectifying his own and his horse's short-comings, and after a lot of mutual hard work emerged at Tidworth filled with optimism. But again the gods were not with him when, jumping across a time-saving corner on the cross-country, they hit a 'grower' and landed upside down. That really did seem to have ruined any chance of being short-listed for Tokyo, unless they could perhaps redeem themselves with a win at either Eridge or Burghley. The eventual win at both events gave the selectors little option, and Richard Meade and Barberry made a last-minute entry into the British Olympic team.

In Tokyo, despite an attack of cholic that prevented Barberry from training during the last six vital days, they stormed across country to take the lead with $3\frac{1}{4}$ points. By the final phase Sergeant Jones and Richard were the only surviving members of the team, and the bitter disappointment of Britain's elimination only added to the difficulties caused by rough going and inexperience in jumping show fences. Three fences down, plus time faults, relegated Barberry to eighth in the final placings. If the show jumping phase had cost them the individual gold in Tokyo, Richard set out to ensure this would not happen again when he was included in the team for the 1965 European Championships in Moscow. But this time, although the dressage and show jumping went well, Barberry spoilt the record with a stop across country.

Compensation for that lapse came with winning the silver medal at the first ever World Championships at Burghley in 1966, where Richard, the only male in the team, offset moderate marks in the dressage with a maximum bonus in phase 2.

In the next year at Punchestown Britain won the European Champion-ships for the first time since Copenhagen, but although team members, Richard and Barberry were not concerned with the final result. The horse's efforts to put his Irish blood to good effect by banking a steeplechase fence resulted in a crashing fall. Despite a painfully cracked collar-bone his rider carried on to score the fastest time on the cross-country course, and they completed the show jumping on the last day, but their score was not needed in the final summing up.

While Barberry was rested throughout the early part of the 1968 season, Richard had the ride at Badminton on Turnstone, an excellent performer across country with which he had won at Liphook and Eridge the previous year and taken sixth place at Badminton.

This time he and Turnstone finished second to Jane Bullen and Our Nobby, and Richard found himself in the enviably strong position of having two good potentials for the Olympics in Mexico, and the near certainty of being selected.

To be fatalistic is a necessary if difficult virtue of the first-class horseman. Again Barberry fell, this time in the final team trial at Burghley, and in that agonizing moment when the horse's feet slipped as he took off over big rails in a dip, to somersault and break three ribs and his sacral vertebrae, Richard knew not only the anguish over a beloved horse, but in one moment the shattering of all the efforts and hopes and dreams of the past four years. Barberry recovered, but his eventing days were finished, and in the meantime the fates had not finished with his rider. Turnstone went lame, and suddenly Richard Meade was without a horse.

Brigadier Gordon-Watson's generous offer of his potentially great but then still relatively inexperienced Cornishman V, did much to soften the double blow. Immensely impressed after the first few rides, Richard was correctly predicting the horse's great future, but if Lieutenant Jones had little time in which to strike up a partnership with his substitute horse, Richard

Meade had even less. Yet when the time came both The Poacher and Cornishman showed their Olympic worth, and their riders gained a place amongst the world's finest horsemen. With a little luck either might have achieved the bronze individual medal, but the glory lay in helping to bring back the team gold to Britain under the unimaginable weather conditions that will always make the Mexican Olympics memorable.

There was another rider in Mexico who might, on two counts, have ridden as a member of the British team. This was Mark Phillips, then an officer cadet at Sandhurst, who had been on the original short-list. When, like so many others, his horse went lame, Mark flew out as nominated reserve rider, a position allowed under Olympic rules whereby a National Federation may field one substitute. In an emergency this rider can be called on to replace a member of any one of the three equestrian teams representing their country in dressage, or in show jumping, or in the three-day event. Obviously the rider selected for the job is thought to be capable of 'filling in', at Olympic standard, in all three categories, and therefore considered to be an all-round horseman of outstanding ability. It says much for Mark's talent that, when the original substitute fell out through illness, at twenty years old he was then the chosen man.

Like Jane Bullen, with whom he had been a co-member of the Beaufort Hunt branch of the Pony Club and co-team mate in the inter-branch horse trials, Mark was a quick mover in the eventing world. His prowess was furthered by having Lieutenant-Colonel Weldon as his Pony Club instructor, a notable horseman who was one of the 'giants' of eventing in the early days, rode in the 1956 Olympics and is now a director of the Badminton Horse Trials. After leaving school in 1966, on the Colonel's advice, Mark went, for the first of many times, for a period of training to Bertie Hill, another member of the 1956 gold medal winning team in Stockholm, who now runs a successful and well-known training stable in Devon.

In retrospect, the assessment of Mark Phillips is as a born 'natural', one of the best and easiest pupils to have visited the farm at South Molton. Mark was then about seventeen, and had only been there a short while when he was asked to try his hand with a difficult, if able horse, with which no-one else was having much luck. Mark climbed into the saddle, popped the animal over a fence or two, and the horse 'went like a dream!' Asked for his solution, his reply was concise: 'Mustn't interfere,' he said, 'Leave it to him ...' an illustration of the enviable, instinctive understanding this rider has of a horse as an individual, and of his good fortune in being able to get on any horse and it will go for him, be it novice, intermediate or advanced grade. When Mark Phillips is competing, more often than not he is the man you have to beat.

Mark entered Sandhurst in September 1967, and in that same month rode at Burghley in his first three-day event. His horse was Rock On, a 16.1 h.h. seven-year-old bay, with which he had won or been placed in every one-day trial he had ridden in the previous season. Although a magnificent jumper, Rock On was still inexperienced and also a 'bit of a nut case', and until years added some discretion, almost impossible to hold across country, then a matter of small moment to his rider who was equally young and carefree.

The pressures at Badminton in 1968 were, as always in an Olympic year, greater than usual, and on the results depended which riders and horses would be asked to form the short list. Jane and Our Nobby were first, narrow winners over Richard Meade and Turnstone, with Ben Jones and the ill-fated Foxdor third, Mark and Rock On fourth, and Derek Allhusen with Lochinvar fifth. These, with four others, were listed, but so many of the horses went lame that only two of the originals survived for the team. Rock On strained a tendon just before the final trial at Burghley, and so Mark's horse, which eventually died under an anaesthetic before there was time to prove his true greatness, was selected to train for the Olympics he never attained, while his rider made the grade to get to Mexico, even if he did not ride there.

While those riders who had made their way to the top were winning honour for their country on the other side of the Atlantic, others whose names would one day become famous were still down at the bottom, or had not yet started on the long slide that could, so easily land them back at the start not once, but several times.

Lucinda Prior-Palmer, then fifteen, was making a first, not entirely favourable acquaintanceship with a spooky, turbulent young chestnut called Be Fair. Virginia Holgate was still living abroad and oblivious to competing in any form. Janet Hodgson, Sue Hatherly and many of the other names in combined training that were to become household words, were either still at school or in the process of leaving. Princess Anne was just embarking on the world of adult competing.

By the spring of 1968 and before she left school in that July, the first big steps had been taken towards furthering Anne's ambition to make combined training her chosen sport. For a start, she needed a horse.

There was obviously no material reason why Anne's first event horse, or any subsequent one for that matter, should not be a fully experienced, highly schooled animal, already qualified to 'schoolmaster' her way into the sport, except that Anne, like all her family, prefers to do things for herself. She is just not interested in having things presented to her 'on a plate', and at the suggestion of Sir John Miller, the Crown Equerry, her first would-be eventer was one of the many good animals bred by his own Stella, Bertie Hill's mount in the 1952 Olympics, that had hunted a little, but was totally inexperienced in any form of competing. Purple Star is a 15.3 h.h. bay gelding. At five years old he had promise and quality, plus the personality, and ability that still persists, to tease his rider at the most inopportune moments. He would be lacking in size for a rider as tall as Anne in the big events, but as a change-over from pony to horse and at that crucial stage in Anne's career, this was just the animal. At least that was the opinion of Alison Oliver, the wife of the international show jumper Alan Oliver, who had been asked to help the Princess with her eventing aspirations and her judgement was sound.

While Anne was in her last Easter term at school, Purple Star was sent to the Olivers' stables at Warfield, near Windsor, and Alison rode him in a couple of novice horse trials as a try-out. Directly term ended the Princess began spending as much time as she could with her horse and trainer, and that was the beginning of a lasting and most rewarding pupil-instructor friendship.

Few people could be better qualified for the job than Alison Oliver. As quite a young child helping around the stables near her home, she acquired the knack of considering horses and ponies as individuals, each requiring different treatment and a different degree of understanding. She developed a taste for eventing with the West Lancashire branch of the Pony Club, and passed her Assistant Instructor's certificate when she was seventeen.

In her first job Alison worked for an employer who shared and developed her own interest in trying to assess why various horses and ponies behaved as they did, and was also willing to enter in her enthusiasm for eventing. The flair for getting on with difficult horses and schooling them with success brought more opportunities for competing, soon at three-day event level. These chances increased when Alison went to work for Mrs Gold, the international dressage rider and judge, who was running the establishment at Brookfield Farm with Lars Sederholm, another big name in the training world. When he left to set up his own centre, Alison stayed on to run the stables for Mrs Gold. Soon she was competing more than ever before, and a twelfth place in the 1966 World Championships with the intractible Foxdor, brought her training ability even more to the fore, and the request from the

Combined Training Association to prepare the horse as a possible for Mexico. As she began to concentrate on training horses and their riders, the competing side of Alison's life gradually diminished, and when she became Princess Anne's trainer and took on all her horses, there was not much time for anything else.

Anne started competing with Purple Star during the Easter holidays, at first in Pony Club trials which went very well. The first adult competition was in the novice section of a one-day event at Windsor at the end of the holidays and the Princess was delighted to come eighth. By the time the spate of autumn trials came round she had left school and could concentrate on training with Alison, and riding in every novice section of one-day horse trials she could fit in. She and Purple were consistently placed and by then she had a second string in Royal Ocean, a 16.2 h.h. thoroughbred that was a reliable performer but just lacked Purple's attractive sparkle.

Already on the scene but as yet an unknown quantity, was the chestnut Doublet, bred by the Queen and intended, until he grew too big, as a polo pony for Prince Philip. Doublet was destined to be the horse with which Anne formed the relationship of mutual confidence which quickly took them to the top of the eventing tree. Anne had her first inkling of the suddenness with which a promising event horse's career can end, when Royal Ocean, that most reliable of jumpers, refused three fences at Chatsworth and was retired, both from that event and from further competing. In 1974, when Doublet broke a hind leg during a quiet canter at Windsor and the wonderfully satisfying and successful partnership ended in tragedy, the Princess was to be another who had to face starting at the bottom once more with an inexperienced horse.

The one-day horse trials at which riders start or stay and return to at intervals are either officially financed by and organized on behalf of the British Horse Society, or affiliated to the same body. To be eligible a horse must be five years old or more, a minimum of 15 h.h., and registered with the BHS, the fee renewed annually. The minimum age for riders is sixteen on the day of the competition. If under seventeen they must be members of the Combined Training Group, and if over that age membership of the BHS is a necessity.

Horse trials may include all or any of the four classes, ranging from novice up to advanced, a horse's eligibility determined by its grade. Before 1972 horses were upgraded on winnings, and with prize-money not over-generous it was not all that easy to collect the £15 necessary before leaving novice status, let alone the £40 that upgraded to open or advanced.

Combined training means combined effort – Tidworth Horse Trials, 1972.

Walking the course as you mean to ride it is one of the essentials of eventing – Richard Meade inspecting the depth of the lake at Badminton.

The world of the eventer is a friendly one where the ability to ride and the ability to mix are what counts. Princess Anne and Mark Phillips at the US Horse Trials at Ledyard, 1975.

Some of the suppleness and obedience essential for dressage can be developed on the lunge.

The roads and tracks phase of a three-day event is a test of endurance and timing – Bridget Parker at the Sandhurst Military Academy Horse Trials, 1976.

Dressage is the basis of all good riding – Richard Meade and Gamble performing the test at Badminton, 1975.

Steeplechasing in combined training means that the timekeeper's watch is
your only opponent – Mark Phillips and Brazil at Badminton, 1976.

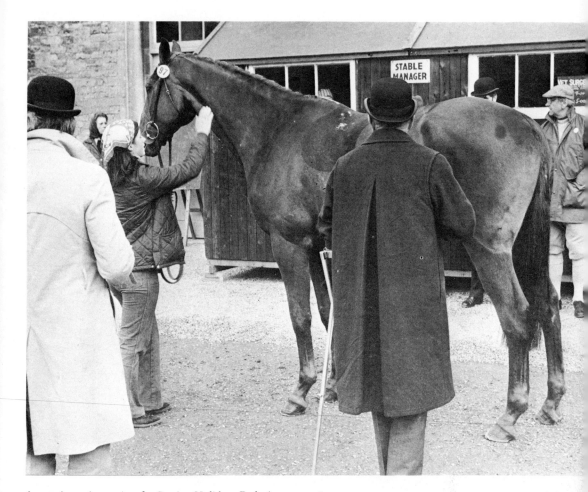

A veterinary inspection for Persian Holiday, Badminton, 1976.

Those precious few minutes of refreshment for horse and rider before the cross country.

Nowadays a points system is used, with so many awarded for the first six placings, the number varying according to the class and whether the competition is a one- or two-day horse trial, or a three-day event.

The eventing season falls into two parts, spring and autumn, with the horses having a short 'let down' in between, and a well-earned rest in the winter. During the autumn season two championship one-day horse trials are held, an open and a novice, confined to selected British-owned horses that have qualified by stated winnings between certain dates in the previous and current year.

The dressage phase, which exerts more influence on the whole competition than in three-day events, the test selected according to the class, comes first in all combined training competitions, but in one-day horse trials the jumping is sometimes included before the cross-country. When this occurs the minimum 30-minute interval allowed each competitor between completing one phase and starting the next, is increased to 40.

The jumping phase of a combined training competition takes place over coloured fences, but otherwise bears little resemblance to show jumping as such. The courses, again varying in severity according to class and competition, are designed merely to test the versatility of horse and rider and, particularly in three-day events where this phase has a great deal of bearing on the results, their ability to cope after the rigours of the previous phases. The courses are simple and straightforward in one-day trials, not more than 800 yards long and with approximately eight to ten obstacles. The height of fences varies between a maximum 3 feet 9 inches in novice classes, maximum spread of 5 feet at the highest point, water 9 feet wide, to the maximum 3 feet 11 inches in height, spread of 5 feet 11 inches and 9 feet 10 inches water, at advanced level.

All combined training cross-country fences are fixed, that is they do not knock down but are constructed to be quickly taken apart in an emergency. Again according to class, the courses vary in length between the novices' $1-1\frac{3}{4}$ miles, with sixteen to twenty obstacles not exceeding 3 feet 6 inches, and up to $2\frac{1}{2}$ miles, with from eight to twelve obstacles to the mile, not exceeding 3 feet 11 inches, with commensurate differences in spreads and water, for the higher grades.

In three-day eventing sustained speed is one of the most demanding factors, requiring not only a bold, fit horse, but one that can cover the ground without having to remain in top gear. The time factor is also an important element in one-day trials, but without the endurance phases of the three-day competition, and with the optimum time for completing the

29

cross-country calculated at 600 metres per minute for the top classes, 525 metres for novices, the required speed is well within the capabilities of the average hunter type.

Horses that compete consistently at the top echelon of one-day trials may be the type that will go on successfully into three-day competing, although this certainly does not always follow. A typical case in point is Collingwood, a full brother to the redoubtable Columbus, that was also bred by the Queen and evented in his early days by Princess Anne. With Alison's help she was schooling both the young greys in the weeks after she and Doublet had come fifth at their first Badminton and the horse was resting. Collingwood never showed quite the same outstanding ability as Columbus, in his early days he was a horse that liked to take a bit of a look before jumping, but he did well for Anne in the novice classes and was upgraded quite quickly – too quickly, his rider thought at the time – to intermediate.

When Collingwood became superfluous to requirements he was sold to John Smart, the show jumper and eventer, who continued competing with him with much success. By then the horse was showing a lot of confidence, he never stopped across country, he had hit the top in one-day events, and then he qualified for Badminton. But when he found himself up against the real big stuff, Collingwood discovered he was not quite the jumper he thought he was. So here is a horse that is superb for competing in one-day trials, the perfect schoolmaster for any young rider coming up into adult events, but just lacking in that extra something needed in the animal that is to go three-day eventing.

Oddly enough the opposite is also true. The three-day eventer being given a freshener in one-day trials at the beginning of a season may even then be so fit that there is nothing about the competition to work off his excessive energies and make him settle. This is also slightly the case with the sprinter and the long-distance runner – the two types are unlikely to shine at each other's sport. The top-class courageous three-day event horse is of such class and quality that he actually needs the roads and tracks and steeplechase before he is prepared to stop pulling and making life difficult for himself, prepared to listen and get down to doing a job of work, which is jumping big and formidable fences and spreads within a tight time limit. And though the indomitable little three-day eventer Dubonnet does not quite fit the category of the 'chasing type of event horse, he seldom won anything in one-day horse trials because he thought the fences not worth the effort!

When it comes to the type of horse that will give his rider fun in one-day trials without much thought of hitting the tops, the scope is wide. A hunter type, perhaps by a premium stallion (which is a thoroughbred), out of a mare which may or may not be half or three-quarters bred, could be the job, but so could something considerably less classy. A horse of the right size, that is comfortable and has the manners and ability to carry its rider safely across country with hounds, would be very good basic material. In the end, given soundness, a good temperament and passable conformation, it is what is done in the way of training that will make the horse into a good, bad, or adequate performer, and this is the chief ingredient in the fascination of the game. Another, the real importance of getting the animal fit for what it has to do, has a side to it that is not always appreciated.

Like most sports and equestrian ones in particular, there is an element of risk attached that adds a flavour, and although no-one wants a fall, this is an accepted hazard. Horses can fall for a number of reasons, but those in combined training, if often spectacular, seldom incur much damage to either rider or mount. The bad falls mostly occur when a tiring horse is being pushed beyond his limit. In a one-day horse trial it is not necessary for the animal to be at the same supreme peak of fitness essential in a three-day event, but time as well as distance still plays a part in the jumping phases of these competitions. A horse that could cope easily with hunting one full day a week is in the right physical shape for completing this type of horse trial. To take a horse into a competition for which it is not physically fit is cruel as well as foolish. Any act of proven cruelty to a horse during combined training competitions is liable to be penalized by elimination on the authority of a BHS steward, and the same penalty can be exercised in the case of a horse that is lame, sick, or exhausted, but the onus of having the horse fit for the day lies with its trainer.

A fit horse also requires the obvious corollary of a fit rider. Like Princess Anne, most of the top-knotch eventers find that the sheer physical effort of schooling several horses keeps the rider in hard condition. During the off-season in the winter those who do not hunt regularly usually find some other method – Lucinda Prior-Palmer plays squash.

In addition to being physically fit, a rider's state of mind is very important. Courage and quick thinking are obvious essentials, but so is the ability to accept the days, either schooling or competing, when the horse just will not settle. It is no good getting fussed or worried because this reacts on the horse, particularly the blood horse that is already 'up tight' with good food and conditioning. If this occurs during schooling the answer is to leave well alone and do something else. If it happens in the dressage arena the only recourse is to remain calm and quiet, kid the horse along as far as possible, and accept that this is 'one of those days'.

3

Ask Bertie Hill or Mark Phillips for their idea of the ideal international or Olympic event horse, and like the majority of those at the top they will plump for something on the lines of Cornishman v or Merely-a-Monarch. Both are big, powerful and athletic thoroughbreds, 'chaser types that would not look out of place in the winner's enclosure at Cheltenham on Gold Cup day, but with an added quickness and cleverness for the different type of jumping required. Both were distinct handfuls in their youth, demonstrating like all great horses the 'little grit' Bertie Hill looks for in his young entry. That is, a horse with personality, that has a 'small nap, but a good nap' about it – which translated means that it is a high-couraged animal with a mind of its own, that will try it on at first, but once it acknowledges you are the better man, will do anything you ask of it.

Both these horses had the ability, in the right hands, to excel in almost any equestrian sphere. Merely-a-Monarch, who hit the eventing scene in the early sixties, is said by those who knew him to have shown all the qualities of a first-class steeplechaser. And at the same time that he and his owner, the brilliant rider Anneli Drummond-Hay, were storming up the eventing ladder, and for good measure winning the 'dressage and jumping' championship at the Horse of the Year Show in both 1960 and 1961, they were show jumping with sufficient success to qualify Monarch as Grade A.

This pair belong to the era before women were allowed to ride in Olympic three-day events, and to that extent were limited in the fields open to conquest. In 1961 a win at Sherborne, their first major event, was the prelude to victory at Burghley. That left only the Badminton Horse Trials as a bastion that fell in the following spring. The exceptional talents of this great horse were then channelled exclusively into show jumping where, if not without vicissitudes, he also won supreme awards at home and on the international scene.

Cornishman v, Richard Meade's replacement ride in Mexico, is a beautifully proportioned 17 h.h. bay with a raking stride. Bought by Brigadier Gordon-Watson in 1963, the four-year-old was destined to be a hunter, a role to which he has happily reverted on retirement.

In youth very highly strung and headstrong, Cornishman had been very difficult to break and was brought on slowly and patiently, without much being asked of him until he was seven. Then in 1966 this exceptionally bold and handsome animal that matched jumping ability with a ground-covering gallop, was run in three point-to-points, only to fade disappointingly after two miles. The cause was later found to be an unsuspected breathing restriction, but in the meantime Cornishman had been taken on by his owner's young daughter, Mary. After a somewhat hair-raising week together on a Pony Club course, despite the horse's size and over-abundance of good spirits, this petite but courageous rider fell for his personality and the challenge he presented. It seemed that eventing might be his *métier*, and with help from the trainer Dick Stillwell, a fourth at Wylye in their first open one-day horse trial gave Mary hope for the future.

In 1967 Cornishman won the working hunter class at the Royal Windsor Horse Show and was Reserve Champion at the Horse of the Year Show in the autumn. Despite jumping out of one dressage arena in an excess of bonhomie, Cornishman's and Mary's eventing prowess was awakening interest. This was strengthened by their winning their first three-day event, the Tidworth Rover Division, in the same year, a victory that confirmed the horse's promise was being matched by performance.

In the following spring, after an intensive dressage course under the expert direction of Ben Jones, Cornishman and Mary continued to impress with their showing in the season's events. Even so, when the horse, after his rider had broken her leg, was so generously offered as a replacement in the Olympic team, he was still comparatively inexperienced. But like that gallant veteran, The Poacher, Cornishman's epic courage and ability in galloping and jumping at Mexico City, under the freak monsoon conditions will never be forgotten.

Cornishman returned home a champion to continue his career with Mary Gordon-Watson. The powers that be were sure of the horse but aware of his rider's comparative inexperience. The pair were not included in the team for the European Championships at Haras du Pin in 1969, but won the individual title there. A year later they followed up by becoming individual World Champions at Punchestown, and members of the winning British team, Cornishman being one of the few horses to go clear over a horrific cross-country where half the starters were either eliminated or retired. Second at Badminton in 1971, they then helped Britain win the European gold, and collected a fourth in the individual placings for themselves.

In 1972 Cornishman achieved the supreme accolade. Ridden by Mary he was included in an Olympic team for the second time in his life. Britain won the gold at Munich, and only one refusal in an otherwise near perfect cross-country lost the individual bronze for Mary and her mighty horse.

It is such stuff as dreams are made of, and unfortunately horses of the calibre of Merely-a-Monarch and Cornishman v belong more to the 'chaser's scene of the big races, and seldom come within range of the event rider or his pocket. But not everyone has the same ideas about what goes into the making of a good three-day event horse, or even on what produces the essential extra spark of those few animals qualified to make the Olympics. What is agreed is that a horse that is always at full stretch in order to make the speed requisite in a three-day event, cannot stay at the top. It may pull off a single effort, but to cope with, not only the gruelling demands of the cross-country after the previous endurance and steeplechase phases, but also those of the last day, when it still has to pull out sound and fit to jump a course of show fences, a horse must always have something in hand. In addition to substance and good temperament, the three-day eventer must have the speed and stamina to be able to cruise, to be the type of horse that is never in top gear. And this is an attribute imparted by thoroughbred blood, although the ratio may vary from horse to horse.

In Munich, in 1972 when the last minute lameness of Debbie West's Baccarat forced a change in the team, the first substitute, Lorna Sutherland's Peer Gynt was by-passed in preference to Bridget Parker's Cornish Gold, because the fast galloping course was better suited to a thoroughbred horse.

In those same Olympics, Major Allhusen's famous Laurieston, with which Richard Meade won the individual gold and was instrumental in the British team win, is the grandson of a German transport mare, of Irish draught type, that probably hailed from Poland or Czechoslovakia. But his mother, Laurien, in 1959 the best event horse in the country, was sired by a thoroughbred 'chaser, and Laurieston himself, like Merely-a-Monarch, is by the thoroughbred premium stallion, Happy Monarch.

On a successful if not quite Olympic plane come the Dubonnets of this world. This is the little horse that set out with Virginia Holgate on the trek to the top by helping her win the individual trophy in the Junior European Championships of 1973. Out at grass and in his winter coat, Dubbonet looks like a hairy little cob with the back end of a bus, and he was bought in Five Lanes Cattle Market in Cornwall, as a sucker, for £35. But although his dam was a very wild part-thoroughbred-New Forest pony cross, Dubonnet has the honour of sharing the same father, Golden Surprise, as Cornishman v, parentage that has imparted one of the stoutest hearts and biggest leaps to be found amongst the present-day event horses.

Jason, the 16.2 h.h. 'bravest ever' horse that Virginia rode to win the 1975 mini-Olympics in Montreal, is a very different type. He is an Anglo-Arab, sired by Pelikan, a now dead Russian Arab, out of a thoroughbred mare. He is an extravagant mover that loves hard going but is not so happy when it is 'sticky' – a heritage of his 'desert' blood – yet had the heart to 'go like a bomb' in Holland when the course had turned to sloshy mud.

Good looks do not always reflect a horse's inner quality, any more than they do with the animals' owners, and in all facets of the horseman's world there are horses of many different kinds successfully doing the same job. Lucinda Prior-Palmer's Be Fair, with which she won Badminton in 1973, became individual champion of Europe, and was first choice for the selectors' short-list for the 1976 Olympics, is a handsome lightweight thoroughbred, oozing quality, versatile, intelligent, and with looks to match his ability. Janet Hodgson's Larkspur comes in quite a different mould. This Irish bred horse stands 17.1 h.h. and is substantial and stocky with it. Now retired he too was a notable event horse with the speed and aptitude to win the Dutch three-day event in 1971 and Burghley a year later, and with courage to equal his rider's when they picked themselves up and carried on after two crashing falls at Kiev in 1973.

The plucky little Baccarat, that has the distinction of never having been ridden by anyone except his owner, lacks the size that many consider essential in a three-day eventer, yet he and Debbie West are among the most consistently placed competitors in the sport.

Princess Anne's famous Doublet was very unlike her Goodwill, the horse that, with Be Fair, was excused the pre-Olympic trials at Badminton in the spring of 1976 as near-certainties for the short-list. Doublet, bred by the Queen, was a good-looking all-rounder by the Argentine Doubtless II, out of Suèrte, one of Prince Philip's ex-polo ponies that was also Argentine bred and therefore all but pure thoroughbred also.

The horse presented exactly the challenge Anne wanted when she was starting her career, and having got the measure of Purple Star needed to progress to something different and with greater potential. Doublet was a very sensitive animal, just beginning to straighten out after a difficult youth, but although Alison Oliver was convinced from the start that here was great horse material, the chestnut took a lot of understanding and was not entirely to Anne's taste when she started riding him. She does however like getting her teeth into a problem, and with faith in her trainer's judgement decided the fault lay more with her than with the horse. Both had a great deal to learn, Doublet was entirely green, but under Alison's guidance the Princess set about forming the partnership based on mutual confidence that was to take them quickly to the top.

Unlike Goodwill, whose impetuous outlook, although now modified, can still make the dressage the most uncertain phase, Doublet showed a flair for it that began to give him and his rider a commanding lead in the novice one-day events in which they were competing, that in 1969 culminated with sixth place in the Chatsworth Novice Championships.

Success in 1970 upgraded Doublet to open, and in the following spring after intense press and public comment on the possibility and desirability, of the Queen's daughter doing such a thing, Anne and her chestnut horse competed at Badminton to finish fifth out of forty-eight starters in their first three-day event. The winner that year was Lieutenant Mark Phillips riding Great Ovation.

At Badminton, like Burghley, the severity of the course varies in ratio to the proximity of the Olympics. It can be a law unto itself, in which one-time-only winners are not unknown, but Anne had no intention of resting on her laurels. Doublet had matured into a co-operative, generous animal that settled immediately to each phase of an event as they came, with dressage above the average, and the ability to gallop well within himself plus the courage to tackle the big fences. But both rider and horse were still lacking experience in three-day events, and whatever her private hopes, Anne was quick to discount press speculation about her being a certainty for the short-list for the 1971 European Championship team. In fact, and within a little while of being asked to ride as an individual, she had to go into hospital for an operation, and that would seem to have put paid to that. But a self-imposed crash course for getting fit in record time, while Alison Oliver continued the vital work of preparing Doublet, paid off, and against long odds Princess Anne became individual European Champion of 1971 and, by vote, Sportswoman of the Year.

Sadly that was to be almost the swan song of a great horse. Off work for nearly a year with what had appeared to be an unimportant bruise on a ligament, the result of a knock on the cross-country at Burghley, despite high hopes of his being fit, Doublet was unable to compete at Badminton in 1972, and that meant no question of the Olympics. Apparently fit to defend Anne's title at Kiev in 1973, Doublet was eliminated at Osberton for a totally uncharacteristic three refusals in the final trials, and Goodwill went in his stead. In the spring of 1974 the chestnut scored only 15 dressage penalties

37

in the Downlands Horse Trials, and in the final results came second, to separate Mark Phillips's first with Columbus and third with Great Ovation. Doublet appeared to be fully recovered and came out at Badminton, but after a bad fall on the steeplechase Anne withdrew him, compensating for the disappointment with a lovely ride on Goodwill to finish fourth to Mark's victory with Columbus.

It is possible that Doublet sustained an unsuspected hair-line fracture in that fall, but within a few weeks a hind leg snapped below the hock when Anne was enjoying a quiet canter, and she lost the good companion with which she found her way to the top.

Anne thought the world of her first three-day event horse, but after nearly two years with Goodwill as first string, she now considers that good as Doublet was and undoubtedly a great horse in his way, this other horse of such a very different stamp has much more scope. Goodwill, bought as an eight-year-old show jumper from Trevor Banks, is a much stronger, tougher animal than Doublet. Where the chestnut was always a gentleman in the stable yet aloof by nature, this horse is friendly and sweet-natured, and normally quiet to exercise, if not alone in keeping something up his sleeve for the exciting moment when his head is turned for home.

This is an animal that now really enjoys his competing. He has calmed from the exuberance of his early days in the dressage arena, when it was useful that Anne had previous experience of coping with Columbus, the powerful grey which as a novice was ready to take off over the 'white boards' with or without the drop of a hat. Goodwill's tendency to gallop with his head low, 'sitting on his bit', used to result in a lot of wearying argument when his rider wished to slow or shorten him for a fence. Now he is ridden across country and jumped in a roller gag with a thick mouthpiece, intrinsically a 'soft' bit but a combination that, with light hands and sensitive approach is especially useful for a girl rider competing with a powerful horse. Anne finds the great advantage of this form of control is that both she and Goodwill are fully aware that she can now stop or slow much more quickly if she wants to, so they no longer fight the issue to the same extent – a satisfactory state of affairs that is time and strength saving, and considerably better for the horse's mouth.

On arrival Goodwill was a Grade A show jumper, but eventing was something quite new. He took to the sport with enthusiasm and without too many problems, and Anne, by then well-versed in bringing on novice horses took little time in getting him upgraded. Her eighth place at Badminton, with only one stop, in 1973, was very encouraging, and she was then allowed to substitute Goodwill for Doublet at Kiev.

Much has been written about the notorious second fence on that European Championship course, and few do not know that Anne and Goodwill were amongst the numerous fallers there. Anne blames herself for choosing the wrong approach to a fence that, had it come later in the course and not been sited at the bottom of a rough-surfaced, slippery hill with a left-handed turn at the end, would have caused little trouble. As it was Goodwill took off too soon, hit a pole, pecked and fell on his head, shooting off his rider to fall heavily on her shoulder and the side of one leg. That landing probably saved breaking a collar-bone, but the leg remained numb and refused to function for a couple of days, while the shoulder was longer in recovering. Anne was not a team member that day, and the 60 penalties incurred for a fall put her right out of the running for the individual placings. Unable to put any weight on one leg, and with an inexperienced horse, having only one three-day event to his credit, that had just fallen for the first time in his life and might well refuse or fall again if taken on without the proper aids – calamities that Anne knew could have far reaching effects – she made her own wise decision to retire.

By 1976 Goodwill's showing in all the events since Kiev were much to his rider's satisfaction. Inevitably there were 'on' days and slightly 'off' days, but overall the horse was coming up to her highest hopes, and if their placing, twelfth to Lucinda Prior-Palmer's tenth in the 1974 World Championship, was at first glance a little disappointing, there was reason for it. On the second circuit of the steeplechase that day Goodwill put in an enormous leap at the open ditch, and then almost pulled up in his length on the stride after landing. Anne thought he had really gone, but after trotting a few paces he went on to finish with only 4 time faults. It was then discovered that the horse had struck into himself, straight on to the back of the tendon sheath with only the leg bandage saving him from more crippling damage. The horse was not lame, but the leg was obviously painful and it was not a very happy pair who set off on the start of nearly five miles of cross-country, with Anne worrying about going at all, and Goodwill lacking his customary enthusiasm. However this horse is as sensible as he is brave, and he protected himself from further damage by not jumping too fast, and pitching straight down over the drops instead of jumping out – a proceeding that gave his rider a few nasty moments, and at the Trout Hatchery, where one leaps down into water, ample opportunity to demonstrate just what a fine horsewoman she is. There was an uncharacteristic stop at the Coffin, the type of combination Goodwill normally finds quite easy, but they finished the day, and under circumstances where a less courageous horse would have 'packed it in'.

In 1975 Britain fielded the first ladies-only event team and sent them to Luhmuhlen in Germany to contest the European Championship. The team consisted of Princess Anne with Goodwill, Lucinda Prior-Palmer with Be Fair, Janet Hodgson with Larkspur, and Sue Hatherly with Harley. They returned in triumph with the individual gold, won by Lucinda ahead of Anne, and the team silver, the gold wrested from them by the Russians, by a narrow margin caused by Harley's calamity with a show jump.

Be Fair's good dressage test stood him in good stead to keep him 14 points ahead of a rather unsettled Goodwill, but both horses were clear in the other phases to finish first and second. Goodwill gave Anne a super ride, with only one moment of anxiety when they were not quite of a mind at the water, and she had the added bonus of discovering her horse could gallop a lot faster than she thought.

Goodwill, sired by the Hunters' Improvement Society's Eventing Trial could well owe some of his strength, as well as his unclassical hunter-type good looks that won him the Working Hunter Championship at Wembley, to his dam, a mare of unknown ancestry that came to Yorkshire from Ireland as a hunter. There are those who do not consider Goodwill an Olympic type, but he has speed, stamina, athletic ability and courage. He is a great horse, and he is also one of the good companions with which Princess Anne and her husband share so much mutual interest and pleasure.

Unlike Mark, Anne is not a committed lover of the one hundred per cent thoroughbred for the sport. This could be due to the somewhat ambiguous relationship she has with her own Arthur of Troy, a well-bred one-time racehorse that is one of her two second-strings to Goodwill. The horse quickly graduated to open and went well in America in 1975. He is obviously brim-full of ability, but Anne somehow finds him disappointing and a not altogether enjoyable ride. She considers he is lacking in concentration, and contrary to popular opinion, describes Arthur as one of the most stupid horses she has come across. This outlook is heresy to Mark, and one which his wife admits may be due to her and the horse being mentally incompatible!

The Princess's feelings are very different about Flame Gun. She thinks a lot of the 'hot little chestnut number' that is in some ways like Goodwill, but with the much quicker acting braking system across country that makes him an easy ride at speed. He, too, has a lot of ability and is a great character, a cocky little show-off, that without being in the least nappy has a temper, occasionally demonstrated by stamping his feet at inopportune moments such as the middle of a dressage test. Unfortunately Flame Gun seems more prone to injury than most – both he and Arthur went lame within a week of each other before 1976 Badminton – but Anne does have a lot of fun and success with this horse. Whether he ever matches up to Goodwill, that horse in a hundred, is a matter for the future.

This leaves Mardi Gras, like Flame Gun an open horse, though both Mark and Anne appear a little bemused by the fact. Sired by the Queen Mother's great steeplechaser, Manicou, his dam a hunter, Mardi Gras was a wedding present, at the time a four-year-old and a distinct handful.

Anne took him in hand, and after two horse trials when he was five, the little horse, still on the 'bolshy' side, was given extra work as a cure and attended his next competition after being out with the drag hounds three days previously. There was a distinct improvement, and on their next outing, a cross-country race, Anne was surprised by the chestnut's enthusiasm. Sent away for some weeks hunting, stories of Mardi Gras' expertise over five-barred gates and other horrific obstacles filtered back to please if surprise his owners, and in the following spring Anne restarted him on the eventing round.

Their good efforts in a one-day trial where he was going across country like a train, were literally dampened by the chestnut's unco-operative way of jumping into water all four legs together, a method that dunked his rider in the drink, but despite such minor vicissitudes, Mardi Gras' progress in eventing was on the up. Anne fell off him again that spring, but by the autumn he was going well and despite poor dressage marks, came up with two second places. He won his first intermediate, where it is said his performance matched his looks, and at Bramham, his first three-day event, they were third, with only a moment's lack of concentration at one of the easiest fences on the cross-country depriving them of a win.

Anne is now very pro Mardi Gras, even though she has fallen off him more times than with any other horse. He is another 'fun' character, it has been entertaining work bringing him along, and the way he now goes across country makes it all appear just too easy. It remains to be seen whether he will continue to leap quite so effortlessly over anything that comes his way, once he is faced with the really big fences.

Except for an untried baby, bought in Devon, that Anne and Mark broke and backed themselves, Goodwill, Flame Gun, Arthur of Troy, and Mardi Gras are, as their owner says, 'her lot', although she was hoping to get the ride on Candlewick.

This young mare was bred by the Queen and is by Night Watch, the stud teaser at Sandringham, out of the elderly matron Trim Anne, parentage that makes Candlewick a half-sister to Colombus. But although the mare is described as a somewhat strange lady, she is sweet-natured and calm, by temperament as unlike the tempestuous grey and others of his family, as she is in the looks that have brought her victory in a couple of hunter classes, and the hunter championship at Ardingly Show. The Princess has jumped Candlewick in the ring, and out hunting finds the mare's readiness to stand quietly when nothing is doing, a great improvement on the behaviour of some of her other horses when out with hounds. Mark, who has also hunted the mare, is impressed with her jumping ability. Again, Candlewick's success in combined training lies with the future, and it was very bad luck that in her first event in the spring of 1976 the mare hit a fence and came down, rolling across Anne and giving her a very unpleasant fall.

Mark considers he is very lucky in having had the opportunity of riding so many different horses, a number of them super animals. Has Mark Phillips, like Richard Meade, been offered the ride on so many horses, great and otherwise, because he is an exceptional rider? Or is he an exceptional horseman because he has had the experience of riding so many good and great horses? In fact the two theories are inextricably entwined, and Mark has had his share of ill fortune as well as good luck. He and Rock On were part of the winning team in Munich for the mini-Olympics in 1971, but this was the horse, destined for greatness, that died before it reached its full potential. During 1970, when Rock On was out of action through lameness, Mark had the ride on Bertie Hill's brilliant Chicago with the British team at the World Championships in Ireland, in company with Richard Meade, Mary Gordon-Watson and Stewart Stevenson.

That was the year when inexperience in constructing courses and controlling crowds, combined with appalling wet weather to make the cross-country at Punchestown one of the most calamitous in the history of combined training. When the weather turned sour the course became a battlefield and only four horses, one of them Cornishman, got round clear, and few managed it at all. With Stewart Stevens already withdrawn after the steeplechase, it was a question of 'must' for the remaining three members of the team. They made it, Richard after a heavy fall with The Poacher, Mark after a fall and an unpleasant slip-up on the treacherous going at the most notorious drop fence, and Britain took the title from France, the only other remaining team.

Great Ovation, in part-ownership with his aunt, Miss Flavia Phillips, was

Mark's next horse. Despite all the successes he had with this horse, and no horse wins Badminton two years running without being a good one, Mark does not consider he can be included as one of 'the greats'. He never felt Great Ovation really loved the game, and though, after a best ever dressage in the opening phase of the 1972 Munich Olympics which placed them third, the disasters of the cross-country were not true to the horse's form, the two falls and two refusals over an Olympic but well-designed course, bear out this contention. Mark never places Great Ovation on the same level as Rock On, or Chicago, or that brilliant hope, Columbus.

Through the years when Colonist ii, once Sir Winston Churchill's illustrious steeplechaser, was standing at the Sandringham Stud, he fathered many good and great horses, most of them inheriting their sire's stamina, jumping ability and courage, in addition to a touch of his rough, tough character. The majority of these have tried their fortunes on the race course, many with distinction, but Columbus, a huge and powerful young grey, went to Alison Oliver as a potential event horse for Princess Anne. He was always a handful and over-strong for a girl rider, but his jumping was so brilliant that it was worth spending all the time and trouble and patience needed to get him to co-operate in dressage. As his efforts in this phase improved, Anne had fun and success in competing with the big horse in one-day trials and was ever more hopeful for the future. In 1972, with Doublet out of action, she took Columbus to Burghley, the horse's first three-day event, to defend her right to the Raleigh Trophy she and Doublet had won the previous year. The grey put on a really good dressage test, but at the peak of fitness necessary for such a competition, took such powerful hold on the steeplechase course that he was uncontrollable and the Princess had to pull out.

Without doubt this is a man's horse, and in 1973 Mark took him over. He was also more than impressed with Columbus's ability and potential, but there was no instant partnership. Still difficult and headstrong, the horse gave his new rider several nasty falls that season including two at Badminton, one of those a real 'purler' at the second Luckington Lane crossing, the other into the Lake. But a lot of hard work put in by Alison Oliver during the following winter, and by Mark whenever military duties would allow, resulted in the rider coming to terms with his horse. In the spring of 1974 faith in Columbus's potential was justified.

The horse carried Mark to victory at Badminton in the manner of a champion, tackling the big fences with all the verve and enjoyment of the exceptional animal, never extended yet eating up the mileage on the cross-country with ease. Here, if ever, was an Olympic horse in the making. In the autumn the pair were included in the World Championship team as of right, and they set out for Burghley and further fields to conquer.

Columbus did not settle too well in the dressage, but their tenth place after that phase was quickly changed for the better as the big horse, trained to a hair, made little of the miles and tracks, raced with zest over the steeplechase fences, and at last set off on the long cross-country with its cross-section of solid, tough obstacles.

The ride Columbus gave Mark that day more than confirmed his Badminton form. They went clear in the fastest time of the day, collecting only 8 time faults and going into the lead with 8 points in hand. The round looked as splendid as it felt – until the penultimate fence, a trakener with a big log sited over a ditch, when, although they finished the course, Mark had the odd and worrying sensation of the horse taking off on one hind leg as, it later transpired, the ligament slipped off his hock.

Like all riders, through the years Mark has coped with misfortune and disappointment. There was the death of Rock On just coming into his prime, Great Ovation's 'days off' when victory seemed within sight, horses going lame and having to be withdrawn at crucial moments in a competition, times like Kiev when excessive injuries left him without a ride at all. Nothing has hurt more than the injury to Columbus.

It was not only the bitter disappointment of retiring just when, given only a little luck, the individual World Championship seemed within grasp. It was the knowledge that with an injury like this, although time can heal it in a steeplechaser so that it can continue to race and jump, there is the possibility in this case that one of the most brilliant of event horses may never again be sufficiently 'level' in his paces to compete in the dressage test.

By the beginning of spring, 1976, Mark had three promising youngsters and four horses from which to draw possible starters for the crucial Badminton Horse Trials in April. Any two – the maximum allowed – that he chose to ride and which finished strongly in the first five, would be likely to be selected for the Olympic short-list, and he tried them out in various one-day trials before making up his mind. And as with any competitor, his own choice could still be changed by lameness or injury right up to the declaration of starters that closes at 18.00 hours on the day before the start of the event.

The four horses could scarcely be more different. His own Persian Holiday, 'Persi' in the family, is a sensitive but even-tempered thoroughbred that is a beautiful mover with great ability. Mark had a considerable success with him, but pin-firing for slight tendon trouble in 1975 refused to come right for a long while, and the horse was off work for many months. He was sound six months before Badminton, and the swimming therapy, new to Britain, was used in getting him fit. Eventually Mark decided to seek permission to ride Persian Holiday round Badminton *hors concours* as a try out.

Mr and Mrs Mills's Laureate II, a high-class horse that, ridden by Mark, was one of the best newcomers to horse trials in 1973, and with which he trounced the opposition at both Tidworth and Wylye, was out of work with leg trouble for all of 1974. He is a short-coupled, highly-strung 17 h.h. worth of bounce, that has to be tactfully persuaded in the dressage arena to relax and flow, instead of bubbling over with excitement and well-being, but comes into his own galloping and jumping. Mark rode Laureate in a few trials in the spring of 1976, but by April had decided against riding him at Badminton.

The attractive grey Favour is the mare that, when little more than a novice, stormed round Burghley in 1975 with John Kersley, to make that formidable course look easy and to come fourth in the final placings. She has infinite scope and brilliance but is inclined to be a bit 'nutty' one day – working beautifully outside the arena, and then going in to compete with flattened ears, heavy breathing, and the determination to back when asked for a halt – yet always moving like a dream, and quite likely to be relaxed and calm the next time out. Mark's sensitive riding suits Favour, and she was one of his choices for Badminton.

To complete the picture is Brazil. This 17.2 h.h. gelding, said not altogether in jest to be the longest horse in the world, belongs to Mrs Boucher. He was sired by Tiopoletto, his dam Almond, and was reputedly bred in Ireland to win the Derby. In England his career began with a stay with the dressage expert, Domoni Lawrence, partly to get some condition on his then gaunt frame, partly to try and assess any likely training problems. He proved to have a likable personality but is a horse that will not be bullied into doing things, he has to be kidded along, a technique which Mark manages to combine with forceful riding, and he is exceptionally bold.

Originally Brazil was evented by John Smart, being placed in one-day trials and completing Tidworth and Punchestown. When the horse was far from fit John took him to Boekelo, under the impression the Dutch course would be flat and not very demanding. In fact the muddy conditions made it a difficult course, but Brazil went on round as brave as a lion. He was offered to Mark Phillips, horseless at the time through lameness and injury, as a ride at Burghley in 1975, with the thought that if they got on here was a horse that might be Olympic material.

Brazil, like Janet Hodgson's Gretna Green with which he came second, was a last-minute ride, and Mark rode both in the way he rode Bertie Hill's, also unknown quantity, Maid Marion, to victory two years previously, or any other horse with which he is unacquainted. That is by adapting the same basic principles of sensitive hands, strong legs and seat, but playing safe, not knowing the horse, therefore not trusting it to make any of its own arrangements, but riding it every inch of the way, and coaxing, sometimes almost 'lifting' it round, as he did the visibly tiring Brazil to finish a creditable sixteenth.

The weeks of training prior to Badminton decided Mark that his order of preference for competing, in a bid to get a horse or horses short-listed for the Olympics, would be Favour, Persian Holiday, and then Brazil. In the draw however they came out differently, with Brazil first, then Favour, and Persian Holiday third. As the Ground Jury at Badminton insisted that in order not to gain an unfair advantage the last in the draw must be ridden *hors concours*, the lot fell to Persian Holiday, with Brazil going first.

4

Great horses do not always get the jockeys they deserve, top-class riders cannot always achieve comparable horses, sometimes a great horse-cum-rider partnership stays around the top for years, the partners so attuned to each other that when age or injury takes its toll of the horse the rider finds it very difficult to adjust to another.

The perfect horseman, if such a paragon existed, would be able to get on any horse and ride it equally well. He would also utilize the fact, that even if the basis of rapport with one's mount does lie in the seat of the pants, each horse still has to be considered, understood and therefore ridden, not only as an individual, but also as it is on that day.

In the same way, though the broad outline is similar, each horse has to be fed, schooled, and prepared for the gruelling ingredients of combined training competitions according to its own particular temperament and physique. To produce a horse for a competition at the peak of perfection feasible for that particular animal, is the common aim of all event riders, however far short of achievement they may fall. They differ slightly only in the methods employed to attempt to attain their goal.

Virginia Holgate and her mother believe that, given a ratio of thorough-bred blood to produce the necessary quality, the three-day event horse is made rather than bred. To prove the point they acquire many of their young stock as foals, often of very different ancestry and growing up into different shapes and sizes. The material through their hands has included a 17 h.h. throughbred, a smaller seven-eighths thoroughbred, an Anglo-Arab, the cobby Dubonnet with his pony blood, and a thoroughbred-cross-Irish draught mare, all of which have come up to expectations. The key-stone of the Holgate training is implicit obedience right from the start. The foals, handled every day without fail, in addition to the usual compliance for their age, in the box move over immediately as required and would not dream of stepping outside unless requested. As yearlings and two- and three-year-olds the lessons continue, the young horses quickly learning, whether in the stable, leading in hand to the paddock, or when the time comes for hacking about on a loose rein, that if they do as they are told at once, they are praised, and if they do not, they get the equivalent of a wallop. This training is combined with a lot of patience and plenty of time allocated to bringing on each one slowly.

This vital part of the horses' education is undertaken by Mrs Holgate who thoroughly enjoys the initial stages. Virginia, who prefers to cut out the nursery stuff, takes them as four-year-olds, when they are beginning to accept the bit, and ready to start schooling on the flat and finding out what jumping means. She is always amazed by the calm co-operation of a young horse brought up on these lines, when asked to tackle a *cavalletti* for the first time, or to progress to popping over anything asked, from a twig to its first little fence.

Not all the Holgate horses are acquired as youngsters, but the same methods are adapted to individual ages and requirements. Jason, Virginia's 16.2 h.h. Anglo-Arab, 'in the eye' of the selectors for Montreal until his rider unfortunately broke her elbow, was bought from friends as a four-year-old problem. Sent to Germany as a three-year-old, he had been lunged over five feet fences, at which he galloped in a frenzy of excitement, and otherwise schooled by methods obviously not suited to his temperament. On return to England the horse had proved very nervous, and had developed the unpleasant vice of bolting. Well aware she had taken on a real challenge, Virginia began the first schooling session in the middle of a ploughed field, a sensible precaution since Jason, maybe with spurs in mind, took off the moment she put her leg on him. It took two months of hard work before the reins could be slackened without the horse shooting off, but patience and determination, followed by meticulous obedience training, paid off in the end to produce a partner whose co-operation equals his boldness and jumping powers.

The 16 h.h. thoroughbred from America which the Holgates were implored to 'see if they could do anything with', was a much worse proposition. The horse, handsome and able if with a bit of a 'piggy eye', had never been taught obedience in any form, and allowed to get away almost literally with murder. Since arriving from the States it had half killed its girl owner and put another rider in hospital, and had scarcely been out of its stable since. After discovering the hard way that when she put her leg on this horse it promptly exploded, only to refuse to move at all when she tried again, Virginia employed the expedient, both on the road and in the field, of keeping her leg on it all the time. This resulted in a half hour while the animal went berserk, but usually it then condescended to settle to a degree.

Cautiously the schooling proceeded to include some low fences. The animal was obviously a brilliant jumper and all went well until the day it decided to demonstrate its 'killer' tactics. They had just taken a parallel when the horse suddenly refused point-blank to come round to the right. With its head pulled round almost to Virginia's boot, it proceeded flat out for a high white rail with a bank beyond. It was a terrifying moment because Virginia knew this was the manoeuvre that had seriously damaged his previous riders, and it was only at the last second she was able to whip him to the left, so close to the rail that his quarters crashed against it. Incredibly, a second try produced exactly the same reaction. Scared but determined, at the third attempt Virginia hit the animal as hard as she could on the left shoulder, and it at last acquiesced in turning right.

The horse's re-education continued with alternating short schooling sessions with Virginia, whose love of the game inspires but also excites her horses, with the relaxing, calming effect of work ridden by their placid girl pupil, under the unremitting guidance of Mrs Holgate. When he worked well and obediently, walking and trotting for an hour on the road, or on circles and over *cavalletti* and poles in the field, the horse then returned to his stable for a feed of the high protein grass nuts that seemed to suit his difficult temperament. The training continued for six weeks, then came the reward. This unridable horse that, at seven years old for the safety of its riders had never previously been jumped outdoors, was sold to Holland and four days after arrival completed a three-day event, going clear in each phase.

Unlike Janet Hodgson and the majority of event riders, who hunt their horses to teach them to cope with whatever comes and to act as a 'freshener', poor hunting country precludes the Holgates from utilizing this excellent form of training. Hunting also helps to get a horse fit, especially the youngster that is much more difficult to get fit for the first time, than the experienced horse prepared each season up to the required peak.

At the Holgate stables and most others, training for Badminton, which comes in the first week in April, commences on 1 January. The programme for the three-day eventers is geared to a slow build-up of work through three months or so, to a maximum three hours per day for the duration of one week. As always, the majority of the work consists of walking on the road, trotting only up the hills, and utilizing the steep coombes in a nearby wood for up and down work at all places, culminating in a peak of twenty minutes trotting, eventual cantering, maybe twice a week, for the same length of time, and finally with a weekly gallop.

Dressage schooling is incorporated in the day's work, but the actual schooling in the field is played by ear and varied to suit each horse's physical requirements and mental outlook. Dubonnet is justifiably convinced he knows his job. Given more than one short session per week, spent brushing up on maybe a couple of movements, and he starts fooling around, shying at a dock leaf or responding to the aid to walk by immediately cantering, his expression saying as clearly as words: 'Walk? What d'you mean, WALK?!'

Jason is as unlike Dubonnet as he is from his former self. In the unlikely event of being asked to school in the confines of the field for four hours on end, he would continue to plod round without protest, and since he does need this work he is given four sessions a week.

As a pure thoroughbred, the big, black Tio Pepe is often mentally keyed up and has to be studied and treated with some care (schooling maybe three times a week). He has a good idea of what he is about, but before the dressage test in a competition is always first lunged for a while, so that he can get rid of his inner tensions by bucking and squealing and playing up. When Virginia then gets into the saddle Tio Pepe is prepared to work.

So much for the sensible and elastic programme adapted to three individual horses, but one rule does apply to all and is rigidly enforced. All schooling sessions must end on a good note. If a horse is doing as required and going well at the end of five minutes, then the session finishes. If at the end of an hour it still has not trotted even one circle correctly, then the schooling goes on until it does. The Holgates are convinced that continuing for any length of time when things are going well does nothing but sour the horse, and that the animals do learn to connect quick co-operation with a quick end to school for that day.

Schooling over fences is kept to a minimum. All the horses benefit from being turned out at times in a paddock where a formidable Devon ditch demands jumping to reach the other half of the grazing. The young ones are also gradually taught something of cross-country requirements from ditches in other fields, where a couple of log-piles and a coffin have been constructed, and an assortment of jumps in a wood are used for a change of scene. Twice a year, in the spring and autumn, the advanced horses are taken to Wylye where there is a wonderful variety of every kind of fence, just to get them into their stride once more. The five-year-olds go there more frequently to get acquainted with the type of obstacle they are likely to meet in their first competition. And novices and experienced horses alike are rewarded for a good schooling session with popping over a fence or two for fun. At intervals they go up into the woods to forget all about training and have a 'jolly'.

No jumping is done over anything approaching a show jumping course, but is of the gymnastic type. They do a lot of grid and *cavalletti* work, and over fences comprising one stride before an upright, or bounce fences, no more than 3 feet high, all depending on what stage the horse has reached and, once more adapted to individual requirements. Dubonnet needs more combinations of a *cavalletti* followed by a spread than Jason, who has cleared a length of 28 feet over a 'chase fence. But he finds the *bascule* more difficult to perform and is worked over more of the *cavalletti*-cum-upright type of fence.

The proof of the pudding is in the eating, and apart from other successes, Dubonnet, Jason and the younger Tio Pepe demonstrate that the methods employed by the Holgates pay off. And amongst evidence for the future, at present grazing the paddocks round the house but soon to start on their competitive careers, are the two full brothers to Dubonnet and Jason.

The Devon trainer, Bertie Hill, in his youth a successful point-to-point rider, learned his dressage from that great horseman the late Tony Collins. He rode in the 1952 Olympics, helped to win the team gold at Stockholm four years later, and trained the British teams that won in both Mexico and Munich. He now runs the well known training establishment for riders and horses at Great Rapscott Farm, South Molton, where he copes with his own young horses as well as other people's, and is one of the essential 'men in the background' behind the majority of the top-notch eventers.

Sometimes he has to accept a dash of other blood as well, but through his racing interests Bertie is essentially a dedicated thoroughbred man. Blood lines, particularly those of the sire, he finds important even in an event horse, and when he sets out to buy he likes to know what he is getting taking trouble first to acquaint himself with the animal's breeding.

There are many years of achievement backing up Bertie Hill's training methods, and he sees no reason to deviate from the pattern. The youngsters are broken in the autumn when they are three, then turned away for the following summer. They come up again that autumn and are then hunted, and although it is not good hunting country they do gain the invaluable experience of going across country that the rigours of continental winters deny the European competitors. The seasons with hounds continue after Christmas, but at the same time the horses are learning something of dressage, spending a short while in the indoor school several times a week.

Spring brings the first schooling over fences, *cavalletti* initially, then small spreads and graduating to Bertie's variety of obstacles, dotted around the farm on the sandy soil that allows jumping across country all year round, and with the advantage of a stream running through the bottom meadows. The surrounding steep, hilly terrain is another big asset, and here the horse not endowed with natural balance soon acquires the art of cantering up and down hill as easily as the animal that is.

With this type of schooling and exercise, allied to the feeding of plump, home-grown oats, first-class hay and little else, the quantities varied to suit each horse's needs, the novice horses are fit and ready, physically and mentally to compete in their first one-day trial, mostly as five-year-olds but sometimes a year later. Occasionally the forward animal goes in the spring but usually it is in the autumn that it does a couple of trials as a preliminary to Tidworth the following spring. If a horse is going to make the grade as a top-class event horse, then it is expected to be placed in that first competition. Bertie Hill firmly believes that either a horse has 'it', like the future great swimmer who shows his talent as a child of four, or it has not, in which case, as far as this establishment is concerned, it is best forgotten. Bertie Hill's interest lies with the horse that has innate talent, the one that finds it all comes easily, believing that schooling should only need to be a polishing up of what is natural to the animal. The mare Favour, with Mark Phillips, a contender for the 1976 Olympic team, came third in her first ever competition. She was brought along specially for the big events, and since her trainer is convinced that far too much in the way of frequent competing is asked of the good horses, Burghley, where she came fourth, was only the tenth competition in Favour's entire eventing career.

When it comes to training his riders, Bertie Hill teaches more on the lines of a private lesson than a riding class. He rarely has more than four pupils at a time, never more than six. From May round to winter the indoor school is seldom used, and the schooling goes on in a huge flat meadow at the lowest level of the farm, where there is room for twenty dressage arenas. Each pupil has his own patch to train on, and the individual problems are sorted out by Bertie, who always teaches from a horse, riding up alongside and demonstrating how to remedy the trouble, a method that produces very quick results.

Much of the Bertie Hill philosophy is incorporated in the training methods used by Captain Phillips and Princess Anne with their horses. From the time he first left school, Mark took himself and various horses off to Rapscott whenever other duties would allow, and since marriage he and Anne have been down with their animals to avail themselves of the help and facilities that are always to hand.

One joy of living at Sandhurst that is particularly appreciated by Anne, is that the horses in work at any particular time are stabled right there, next to the house, and that is something she has never known as an adult. She and Mark can now pool their knowledge, and since the Princess and her horses were trained by Alison Oliver, their animals have the benefit of the methods and wisdom of two of the top trainers in the country.

In 1968 when Princess Anne first went to Alison Oliver, she arrived with the assets of good natural balance, a seat that had only to be altered slightly, and, from the trainer's point of view, the heartening ability to take in quickly and act on what is being put across, that is an inheritance from the Queen. She was also quick to appreciate the feel of a horse, and showed a natural rhythm in her riding and the instinct to leave a horse alone and not niggle it. On the other hand, although Anne has always been happy and assured on horseback and most animals go well for her, and she had had the valuable experience of riding different types and sizes at Moat House Riding Establishment, she had no technical knowledge of any kind. She had never had the opportunity to study the essential training and schooling of horses, let alone put it into operation. She knew nothing of the techniques of riding required at the higher levels of eventing, little of the demands, physical and mental, of the sport that she had chosen. Even the tack with which she arrived was unsuitable.

Until marriage the Princess's horses remained with Alison Oliver while their owner came to the stables as often as she could, often getting up early to fit in a schooling session before dashing off to perform some public duty. She could never spare the same amount of time as other competitors for preparing for an event, and had to condense a lot of work into the relatively few hours available. But it was all highly enjoyable and produced satisfactory results. There was no room for ceremony in that relaxed atmosphere as the Princess, under Alison's guidance, schooled Doublet over fences, or they worked together in the indoor school, endeavouring to find tactful ways of restraining and rechannelling Columbus's impetuous efforts to evade some movement required in a dressage test. Trainer and pupil worked in friendly harmony whatever the prescribed programme for the day, and at one moment Anne could be found helping a girl groom unsaddle one horse and tack up another, the next clomping off up the road by herself to meet Alison in the jumping field. But while there was never any question of a trainer doing all the preparatory work, for a rider just to climb on the horse's back and press the correct buttons to compete, life at that time made it quite impossible for the Princess to do more than take a share of the schooling and training. She has numerous royal commitments, there were occasions when she was abroad on royal visits, there were the weeks she was in hospital, and these were times when Alison had to take over the horses completely. These were also the occasions when Alison had cause to be thankful that one of her pupil's great assets as a horseman is the ability immediately to take over at whatever stage a horse has reached in its training, then carry on from that point.

Today both Anne and Mark are still very busy people. The Princess has an increasing number of public duties, her husband is a very keen and conscientious serving officer, and neither of them can spare the same time for their horses enjoyed by most of their fellow competitors. Alison Oliver continues to train the Queen's horses at Brookfield and helps with any of the others as required, but Anne has discovered another facet to her sport. Like everyone else in the equestrian world she now has the source of her and Mark's shared interest and enthusiasm, normally a complement of six horses between them, stabled at their home and subject to their own individual care and planning.

When she has the time Anne can, and does, lend a hand with anything connected with the horses and the day-to-day stable chores, and is as dab a hand at putting on stable bandages or taking her turn with the clippers as she is at facing the judges in a dressage arena. On the mornings when she and Mark are working the horses, the day usually starts with the weighty problem of deciding who will do what. If the schooling is to be at home, then between them they will probably give each horse half an hour on the flat, before handing it over to one of the girl grooms for an hour's exercising hack. Sometimes they box a couple of horses to Windsor to do faster work on Smith's Lawn, but they do make sure that they fit in the horses' actual schooling themselves, and no-one else is allowed to canter or jump them.

These two find that riding each other's animals is a big help. They find the foibles of the other one's horse less irritating than those of their own. And though as top-class riders they have the same aims in view and their riding does not differ in essentials, the mere fact of Mark being so much heavier, and so much stronger in hands, and legs, and seat, can have a different effect upon the same horse. If one of Anne's is being a bit strong and 'bolshy', Mark can set about it and, as his wife puts it, drive it potty for ten minutes until it decides it's just not worth while! Then, battle over, Anne can get back on and the work will proceed much more smoothly. Conversely, if Mark's weight and strength starts reacting on a horse that is feeling ultra-sensitive that day, Anne's approach will help it relax and go more easily for her. Occasionally they compete with each other's horses. Anne rode Mark's

Persian Holiday in the Crookham Trials. When she was off riding after a fall in 1976, her husband rode Mardi Gras at Locko Park Horse Trials, and came second in another section there with Arthur of Troy.

They have enjoyed the fun and interest of breaking in and backing a youngster themselves. They believe in the good effects of hunting on both horses and riders, and consider swimming as beneficial to horses as it is to humans. Often any one of their horses recovering from leg trouble is sent away to combine normal work on the Downs, with two- to ten-minute sessions of a form of therapy long popular in Australia and the States.

Like everyone else in the game, Mark and Anne keep their skeletal training programmes elastic, choosing with care, though sometimes at the last moment, the one-day trials likely to be of benefit to different horses at various stages. When some competition seems to fulfil requirements they set off, usually sharing the driving of the horse box between them, and finding it a chore when most of the horses are involved and they each have to take charge of one of their two vehicles.

One of the great assets of husband and wife sharing the same pastime is that neither has to make sacrifices, going along for company when they would rather be elsewhere. Anne and Mark consider it gives a big edge to fun of the day to be competing in the same trial, even if as sometimes happens, the different requirements of their horses means they are riding in different sections. Usually it seems to work out that on a day when one of them has done well the other has been eliminated or met with some other mishap, and then on the way home their moods can be at variance – one elated with success, the other distinctly down in the dumps. If they are competing against each other and both going well, Mark considers that while obviously both would like to win, if one has to be beaten then it is better it should be done within the family, so to speak! – a viewpoint not entirely shared by his wife, who says she only manages to beat him once in a blue moon, and when she does he is far from appreciative! However, Mark has the last word in that joke, by protesting that he is always pleased when Anne wins – because then she is so pleased herself that they have peace!

These are two competitors with just the right attitude towards what is, after all, a sport. When the heat is on in some big or international event they are as dedicated, as out to win as anyone in the game. But there is still time for the funny moments – such as the startled lady, discovered round the corner of a wood on the cross-country, who leaped to one side of the track while her dog, attached by a long leash dashed to the other . . . and the only way for a galloping horse was to jump between them over the lead!

Competing in the big events is always a nerve-racking occupation for those waiting to start, and for years Princess Anne had also to cope with the urgent attentions of photographers adding to the moments of stress. And while it is entirely understandable that the Queen's only daughter competing at the highest levels in an apparently hazardous sport should have made irresistible 'news', it did not make any easier the Princess's efforts to concentrate on riding in, before a dressage test, a highly-strung, over-sensitive potential equine bombshell. The horses also failed to understand the distracting appearance of a photographer, often an amateur, just as they were coming in to some formidable obstacle on the cross country.

Nowadays the press are seldom anything but considerate and co-operative, although Anne is never likely to be able to enjoy the privilege of doing badly in some competition or falling off in the unrecorded peace and seclusion she would probably prefer! But gone is anything even approaching those mad weeks prior to the engagement, when the Princess and Mark Phillips were more or less besieged as they and Alison Oliver tried to school distracted horses at Brookfield. Now the novelty is less, and most of the photographers are the same and through the years have learned something about the sport. Not all of them, either professionals or amateurs, yet realize that if they would only stand still when out to take pictures of horses approaching on the cross-country, the animals would pay scant attention. It is the movement of someone rushing into position that can disturb the animal's concentration at the vital moment of coming into a fence. But by and large the press have come to appreciate that if they stand back and do not get in the way they get better pictures, as they can so easily with the modern telephoto lens, and everybody is then happy. Horses are quite easily distracted by the sound of cameras, but it is not strictly speaking the fault of the pressmen, that when Princess Anne rides into a dressage arena the general public tend to fall silent, and the noise of the cameras becomes more apparent.

One important aspect of eventing that the careers of Princess Anne and Mark Phillips and other top eventers serve to illustrate, is that success depends not only on hitting the top but, what is much more difficult, in staying there. A one-time victory at Badminton will not interest the team selectors nearly as much as riders and horses who are consistently placed throughout the seasons, but whatever the achievement, few make it without the help of trainers who can be turned to when in need.

Lucinda Prior-Palmer is a great believer in doing it yourself as far as possible, but even so has always relied on outside aid when some problem crops up that needs expert sorting out at ground level, and the psychological boost that this gives. As a child she spent two unforgettable weeks with Alison Oliver. Otherwise her chief adviser is not one of the big names in the training world, but a modest disclaimer of any particular knowledge, who yet has the natural flair for sorting out a rider's or horse's jumping difficulties, and for using exactly the right distances between obstacles to produce the desired result.

This particular helper was available even before the day when Be Fair, bought, principally on account of his breeding and looks, as a present for Lucinda's fifteenth birthday, seemed likely to prove an unfortunate choice. The engaging chestnut, now acclaimed as one of the best eventers and most likely Olympic horses in the country, was then a self-willed, hot-headed six-year-old that his new owner frankly loathed. In the beginning he was virtually unridable, at least by an inexperienced teenager, and was soon on the way to being wrecked. Be Fair still occasionally rears if he feels like it, but nowadays that is merely a well understood expression of exuberance reserved for off-duty moments. In those early days the mere sight of a far-off dustbin was the excuse to stand up, swing round and make for home, fast. It took three months riding by an experienced horseman, backed up by a Landrover driven behind with a lungeing whip out of the window, to change his ideas when he tried to whisk round, and generally to improve his manners.

One of the reasons for Be Fair's sustained brilliance is that he combines great care in his jumping with extreme boldness. This is an unusual combination, and handled without tact at the next stage in his education a horse of his sensitivity could well have lost its courage. But Lucinda sent Be Fair for a season's hunting with the Pytchley in the hands of another first-class rider who had the understanding not to attempt to restrain the young horse, shivering with nerves at first sight of hounds, but allowed him to stride on alongside the huntsman and tackle the big fences beside an experienced hunter.

On his return there was need for a lot more patience combined with the right schooling, but from that day Be Fair has scarcely looked back, even if Lucinda's first competition with him left something to be desired. She was then sixteen, and feeling very proud to be showing off to her Pony Club friends with a horse that was already impressive, by riding in the Pony Club Interbranch Regional Trials. Her conceit was short-lived however. It had to be Lucinda that fell off that day, just as it had to be her super horse that managed to get himself inextricably stuck under the fence.

That same year they tackled their first one-day trials under BHS rules in the novice section at Rushall where a seventh place seemed to augur well for the future, and were in the winning junior team at the European Championships.

Badminton 1972 was one of the memorable years in the history of the event. Battle commenced in the dressage arena where Mark Phillips and Great Ovation pulled out all the stops to score 59, seven better than Richard Meade riding the Allhusens' Laurieston, with Mary Gordon-Watson and Cornishman the reigning world champions a mere ·5 behind them. At that stage Lucinda and Be Fair, competing in their first big competition, were lying seventh with a creditable score of 83.

1972 was also Olympic year and the cross-country course was not designed with the maximum size that might ask too much of the horses, but as always presented plenty of problems. Richard Meade with his second horse, Wayfarer, paved the way with what proved to be a deceptively slow looking clear, to lie fourth at the end of the phase. Lucinda set off, with only an added 4·8 time faults in the steeplechase, after a very fast round by Hazel Booth and Mary Poppins and a number of disastrous ones by British and foreign competitors alike.

Be Fair, whose sire, Fair and Square, won Burghley with Sheila Willcox in 1968, was in his element. With only one stop and the third fastest time of the day, equal with Richard and Laurieston, Lucinda and her horse were sufficiently impressive, backed up by a clear in the jumping phase, later to be short-listed as Olympic possibles. The struggle between Mark and Richard for first position ended in Mark's favour, but with only the 1·25 seconds, penalty for an over-careful wide turn at a fence in the final phase, between the two. Cornish Gold, that was such a good top eventer, and whose owner/rider is one of the best across country, came third, Debbie West and Baccarat, fourth. Cornishman fell on the cross-country and dropped back to fifteenth, Lucinda and Be Fair came up to finish fifth.

In retrospect aware that she and her horse were not then ready for the ultimate test, Lucinda is now thankful that they did not in the end make the Olympic team. They finished the 1972 season by winning the Midland Bank Open Championship at Cirencester that autumn, and in the next spring bumped up the record by winning the coveted Whitbread Trophy at Badminton. Their overall form continued through to the autumn of 1975, and they were a strong and obvious choice for the Olympic selectors' short-list in 1976.

At thirteen-years-old, a good age for a three-day event horse, Be Fair is a handsome, compact chestnut, 16.2 h.h. and of immense scope, an athletic type of horse capable of most anything, and with an intelligent 'play it cool' outlook that his owner adores. In 1975 he attended the Horse of the Year Show as one of the stars in the personality parade, and on the first night was distinctly nonplussed by what he found in the arena, goggling at the lights, fussed by the crowds, the music, the clapping and cheers, and was generally upset. Lucinda feared she might have trouble even getting him 'on stage' on the second night, but she underestimated her horse. Be Fair charged up the chute and through the curtains, scarcely able to wait a moment before emerging into the spotlights, to stand rock-like acknowledging the wild acclaim, to play to his audience like the old hand accepting what he knew to be his due.

As befits a horse which knows exactly what he is about, and one who still preserves the talent of combining care with courage, Be Fair, like the majority of the experienced horses, does little jumping in his long, conscientious preparation for the new season. In early 1976, already excused Badminton by the selectors, he came out at a one-day trial just to limber up, and won it to show he was his usual self. He was then given a month's holiday, which seemed to surprise him, with the aim of having him by July at the same peak of his form as he had been in July 1975.

In the meantime Lucinda had plenty to keep her busy. In Wideawake she had a talented second string, with which she won the Dutch three-day event at Boekelo in 1975 without adding to her dressage mark of 46, and planned to ride him at Badminton in the following spring. There was also the less experienced Hysterical to bring along and a promising young horse that had scarcely started.

The training and preparation of all Lucinda's horses broadly follows the outline followed by most of the top riders, but she is lucky in having the use of the nearby 9 furlong tan-track gallops belonging to the racehorse trainer Toby Balding, and her horses can work there regardless of winter frost or the summer hard. For what she insists is most necessary help with dressage, Lucinda goes at intervals to David Hunt, Alison Oliver's ex-pupil who tries for ultimate perfection by varied and sometimes new approaches. Richard Stilwell, who tackles the problems of relative beginners as well as those of riders such as Richard Meade and Mary Gordon-Watson, is another famous trainer who has never worked to a rigid formula, but adapts remedies to the troubles peculiar to each rider and each horse. He has been in the background of Lucinda's competitive life for many years, and it is on his advice that she has gained a wide experience by less orthodox means than many. During the winter months while her horses are resting, Lucinda leaves for somewhere calculated to broaden her outlook, not only in the riding sphere. She has helped to train horses in Greece, and in Iran where she was able to sample the hot but co-operative temperament shared by all Persian horses, whatever the breed. Lucinda is also one who, like Mark Phillips and a growing number of event riders, believes in learning more of the different phases included in combined training, from those who specialize in each particular branch. Mark recently spent a week at Trevor Banks' yard, where Harvey Smith is a partner, and learned more about show jumping in a few days than he has gleaned in his entire riding life to date. In 1974 Lucinda had the enviable chance of two weeks tuition with Hans Gunther Winkler, the German show jumping ace and Olympic medallist, who began his great career in 1952. This was an interesting choice of tutor because, although no-one could question the German successes in international show jumping, their methods, particularly suited to the big, strong German breeds they ride, differ widely from the British, which are individualistic but based loosely on the more flowing Italian style. Herr Winkler however is also an individualist to a degree, a horseman who does not adhere strictly to the more mechanical approach of most German riders intent on the rigid obedience and placing of their horses. He is one of the world's finest equestrians, an international horseman in every sense of the phrase, and he gave Lucinda an insight into the art of show jumping that not only assists in her chosen sport, but has inspired her with an unqualified admiration for his.

Different riders obviously go to different trainers, although the majority usually find their way to the 'top ten' at some time or another, but venue has some bearing on their preference. For those living in the deep south of Devon or Cornwall, there is the expertise of Baron Hans von Blixen-Finecke, the Swedish individual Olympic gold medallist at Helsinki in 1952, able with a shift of weight to get the most unlikely equine to leg-yield within a matter of minutes, and a specialist at sorting out riders' problems at all levels, for all equestrian sports. Robert Hall, who has his well known equestrian centre at Fulmer in Buckinghamshire, and branches in the north and in America, is a leading expert on dressage, and learned his art at *haute école* level at the Spanish School in Vienna. In Oxfordshire Lars Sederholm, a famed event trainer, has a centre where he has developed a system for acquiring all branches of horsemanship, and in the Cotswolds, lucky students of dressage and eventing can go to Sheila Willcox and learn the skills that made her the Badminton specialist of the fifties.

Wherever there is a top ranking event rider, in the background are to be found the trainers who are vital to his success.

Mark Phillips and Columbus on the most
arduous and important phase – the
cross-country – at Badminton, 1974.

At the big events, like the European
Championships at Burghley in 1971, the huge
crowds are a stimulus to the rider but can be
distracting to the horse.

Out in the country when all goes well – Princess Anne and Doublet at
Burghley, 1971.

The moment your horse says 'no' – Miss D. Brands at Tidworth, 1976.

Success – Lucinda Prior-Palmer and Wideawake at the Badminton Lake, 1976.

Failure – Richard Walker and Willgi at the Badminton Lake, 1976.

Bastions of the three-day event!

5

The Danes included Stamford, with Lincoln, Leicester, Nottingham and Derby, as one of the famous 'five boroughs' situated in what was Danish Mercia. Here Danelaw held sway and Stamford became a Viking trading centre, protected by ditch and palisaded mound. The steep slopes on which the town perches must have been easy to defend and provided an impregnable fort from which to sally forth to rout Saxon peasants, even before the seafaring marauders learned to leave their galleys behind garrisoned stockades, and, culling East Anglia's horse-breeding pastures, became if not cavalry at least mounted infantry. And with what relief must even those tough Viking warriors returning from battle, have welcomed four-legged conveyances to carry them back up that hill.

For centuries past any faint remaining echo of the hoofbeats of long-dead Viking horsemen would have been drowned in the characteristic chiming of clocks and donging of bells, sounding from the many church spires that spike the skyline of this ancient town. But in the offshoots of the main street, where timber-framed houses lean confidentially towards each other over the cobbled alleys leading to the river below, it is easy enough to conjure up the shades of horses and riders from decades nearer to our own. Now, in an age when a horse trotting through the rumbling, mechanized traffic in the town could be as out of place as a dodo, horses are yet the reason for the welcome annual influx of visitors and trade that flood into Stamford for a few days each autumn.

At six o'clock of an October morning only some of the shop window displays suggested this fleeting equine interest. There were horses fashioned in felt or plastic, for a while taking precedence over pandas and miniature racing cars at the toy emporium, beautifully created shires and thoroughbreds ousting the other delights of the ceramist's art in the china shop, and in the stationers – horse books for all age groups were well to the fore. To find the flesh and blood creatures themselves it was necessary to walk on down to the river, cross the bridge and the main road beyond, and go on up into the peace and space of the splendid acres of Burghley park.

Once there it is impossible not to be aware of the aura of history that lies between the acres of resilient turf and the centuries-old oak and beech trees that adorn it; unthinkable not to pause and contemplate the breathtaking beauty of the great Elizabethan house, the family home of the Earls of Exeter, seen beyond the lake, its cupolas and crenellated parapets rising up out of the early morning mist. With Badminton, this is the other splendid setting that makes Britain's two major three-day event sites unlike any others in the world.

At that hour there were only an official Landrover or two driving round as forerunners of the nose-to-tail traffic to come, as yet no sign of the crowds that now flock to these events, but which, at least out on the cross-country courses the spacious areas of the parks at Burghley and Badminton can still swallow with ease. On beyond the members' car park and enclosure, the stands surrounding the dressage and jumping arena – the sites where only the dedicated congregate on the two days of dressage, but which are packed to capacity for the final jumping phase – were as deserted as the nearby 'streets' between the rows of trade stands that spring up, mushroom like, each year. Before long these mobile shops would be thrown open to display tempting arrays of saddles and bridles, numnahs, sheepskins, bits and spurs, whips and headcollars; night rugs, sweat rugs and summer sheets; boots, breeches and riding hats; china, etchings, paintings all with an equine theme; horse books and horse food; horse trailers and horse boxes: all and everything that a self-respecting horse or owner could possibly covet, and cheek-by-jowl with a fair sprinkling of wares of more general interest to the common man.

At that hour nothing of this hidden treasure was to be seen, but here and there from behind the tightly-laced canvas fronts snatches of conversation and the delicious aroma of coffee were seeping, to hint at bed and breakfast for the proprietors within. As for the horses themselves, with their riders the chief actors so soon to hold the stage, one or two early risers were being ridden out on light exercise, a couple or more were being limbered up on the end of a lunge rein. The majority were still snugged down in the horse lines, where as always, and as with every detail of the arrangements for running these complicated occasions, the British genius for producing apparent informality goes hand in hand with a smooth-running efficiency, that is the product of long experience and meticulous behind-the-scenes planning.

At the stables a few of the inmates were prudently having a lie-in behind the sacking curtains over the tops of their half-doors, most were gazing with interest at a scene springing to life as girl grooms milled to and fro ministering to their precious charges. Soon there were horses being groomed and horses being plaited, horses eagerly chasing up the last grains of an early breakfast, while a few of the old hands, suffering kindred tension with human athletes not to mention their own riders, were refusing so much as a nibble. Those drawn first to start off on the many arduous miles of roads and tracks, steeplechase and cross-country, were not being given the option – their last feed had been presented five hours or so before.

This was of course speed and endurance day, all the competitors had by then completed their dressage test some two days before, some in the teeth of a freezing, howling gale on the previous afternoon. In the collecting ring warming up under those unpleasant conditions had been Richard Meade with the good young Olympic hope, Tommy Buck, that was sadly to dash all chances of being short-listed with an injury in the following spring. Debbie West was there, schooling her little veteran Baccarat, both beautifully turned out 'pocket editions' that through the seasons have learned their way around most event courses. Aly Pattinson was waiting to compete with Carawich, the pair that were to spring a surprise on some of the forecasters and give the selectors food for thought. Mark Phillips with Gretna Green, a last-minute loan by Janet Hodgson, was riding round under the discerning eyes of Princess Anne, grounded by the lameness of Flame Gun.

The wind grew stronger yet, the cold more brutal, conditions scarcely condusive to a horse's state of calmness that is one of the requisites of the Ground Jury, the panel of three judges who do the independent marking of each movement in the dressage phase. $7\frac{1}{2}$ minutes is the time allowed to complete the FEI dressage tests used on these occasions. The movements consist of a combination of working, medium and extended paces at walk, trot and canter, tracking and half-passes, circles, serpentines, and changes of rein, all to either hand, and interspersed with halts of correctly sustained immobility, a rein back of 5 steps, and examples of what looks deceptively easy, the competitor's ability to trot straight down the centre line.

The judges look for a well-schooled horse that is obedient, fit and keen, and calm. It should have freedom, rhythm, and regularity in its paces, combined with impulsion, the energy that is generated in the hind quarters. The rider is judged on position and seat, and the correct use of the aids. The picture should be one of grace and lightness, the transition smooth, the aids scarcely perceptible, and the horse appearing to do it 'all on its own'.

The standard of dressage required in events is always less demanding than that required in comparable pure dressage tests, where horse and rider are specialists. Event judges would rather see a supple horse performing an elastic test that is, overall, pleasing to the eye, than one being asked by the wrong means to attempt dead accuracy. It is obviously logical that the three-day event rider, as an all-rounder, can reckon on 'getting away with' a bit more in his test than the dressage-only expert, although this does not apply to quite the same extent in one-day trials where the dressage marks exert more influence on the final results of the competition. In all combined training tests 'working paces' have now been substituted for the former 'collected paces'. For while collection, correctly obtained, would never stop a horse from going round Burghley or Badminton excessively well, it is not a necessity in the event horse. The change has therefore been made in an effort to prevent the too frequent sight of some riders endeavouring to collect, by hauling in the front end of the horse and going slow in the pious hope that instead, energy and a tendency towards collection will now more often be created from the back end of the animal.

Whatever might befall them later in the competition, all those fifty-two horses that entered the dressage arena at Burghley that year, were better rides and more able performers for the graduated training they had received in order to participate in the dressage phase. But dressage, much better called training on the flat, is not something that can, or should be compartmented. It is schooling that can change a disobedient, stiff animal into a responsive, supple ride, moving lightly and freely to its rider's wish, and easier, more co-operative and successful whatever its role, be it showjumping, eventing, or what you will. And although most riders include work within the confines of a school or arena, the bulk of training on the flat takes place all the time, exercising up and down hills, on tracks, on roads, or warming up before a jumping phase.

That icy gale that had harrassed the dressage riders on the Friday and maybe accounted partly for some mediocre marks, by the next morning had become a cool breeze, with appropriate mares' tails flicking a blue sky, and only a few ominous clouds piling up on the horizon. The overnight rain had disappeared without trace into the still hard going, any fresh rabbit scrapes on the sacrosanct cross-country turf had been meticulously filled in, and altogether it was a good day for galloping, a good day for the rigours to come.

The first competitors reappeared, now booted and spurred for the fray, and while horses were saddled up and frayed nerves calmed down, snatches of conversation, some of it addressed to the horses, floated out over the stable doors.

'. . . soon as he saw those big parallels, aha he said, I can get my teeth into those! (STAND STILL, YOU!) ... and we soared, literally just soared over them ...' 'He's got his horse twice as fit as ever I could, (Come on, my beauty, open up that mouth!), but can he sit on him?...' '... he turned right, y'know, just as a matter of course, and this year they were turning left! Pity, his dressage's bad enough as it is ...' 'Shivering? Oh, yes, she always gets the shakes ... usually it's the rider! But this lass, she's done it so often she knows what it's all about!'

In one box Debbie West was seeing to Benjie, her first string that day. Richard Meade second to go, was already out and about with Jacob Jones, his other young hopeful, a big horse, slow to develop, whose preparation had to be prolonged, and that by the spring would be, depending on what happened at Badminton, the only Olympic 'possible' for Britain's most experienced rider. In another box Princess Anne was helping one of her girls tack up Brazil for Mark, and wondering why the big brown horse appeared to be finding his hind leg bandages rather strange apparel.

Soon it was time for the first competitor to weigh in before the start of the speed and endurance. Without whip or bridle, but if necessary complete with saddle and any other of the horse's permitted accoutrements, riders have to turn the scales at a minimum 75 kilograms (165 pounds), a regulation that affects the girls more often than the men. Many in fact have to carry lead, in weight cloths that are best hung over special numnahs squared off at the edges, to prevent them banging against the horse. The weight is not distributed in the places that best suit a racehorse for technical reasons.

The formality completed the first to go set off on phase A, the 3 kilometres 960 metres (2 miles 803 yards) of roads and tracks, mapped within and around the park and woodland. The times and distances of this phase vary slightly from event to event and increase in severity according to the standard of the competition, but the rate of penalties remains constant. At Burghley that day competitors were, as always, penalized on roads and tracks by one penalty point for each second in excess of the optimum time (16 minutes 30 seconds for phase A, 33 minutes for the second quota of roads and tracks which comprise phase C). If they exceed the time limit (19 minutes 48 seconds for phase A, 39 minutes 36 seconds for C), they were eliminated.

None of the competitors that day, or at any similar event, would have been able to enter without having previously completed at least two three-day events or advanced classes in two-day trials. No horse would have been accepted unless it was Grade I or II, meaning that it had gained at least 4 points in intermediate or higher level trials, and had completed at least one three-day event or an advanced class in a two-day trial, a minimum of one such competition within the current or previous year.

These most necessary qualifications ensure that the complete outsiders, riders as well as horses, do not somehow get embroiled in a competition far beyond their capabilities, and all those setting off at Burghley that day would have known at least to a degree, what they were about. But for the novice three-day eventer, entered with trepidation for a first competition, probably Tidworth, or Wylye, or the newer Bramham, all designed for riders to get an idea of their and their horses' reactions to the sport, even the phases of roads and tracks can present bewildering problems.

In fact all roads and tracks are set out with kilometre markers, and the harrassed novice wondering how on earth to judge the required speed, has merely to trot the first kilometre fast and be meticulous about noting the time involved. If it takes, say 4 minutes, then that is the guideline, and a walk lasting $1\frac{1}{2}$ minutes can be countered by a $2\frac{1}{2}$ minute canter. Previously walking round all the speed and endurance phases of a three-day event may be an arduous chore – at Burghley it would have involved a tramp of some 14 miles – without the twice-over that all riders give the cross-country, and some the steeplechase as well – but it is a vitally important part of riding such a competition. Footslogging the roads and tracks, in England the tracks predominate, in France the roads, is more an an exercise in learning the way. It means studying and noting down the state of the ground, at what markers the going warrants a short canter to make up for walking a stretch that is rough, or for the brief pipe-opener that most like to give their animals before the end of phase A and the start of the steeplechase. And providing the horse is as fit as it should be, it can be a good plan to push on a little where the ground is suitable, and so have a few moments grace for checking the breast-plate and the like.

The steeplechase course on a three-day event is a lonely place. There is no huddle of other runners, no thudding of other hooves, creak of leather, rasp of breath, admonitions of other jockeys, to lift your heart and inspire your horse. Each fence comes up as another island in a sea of turf without the elation and spur of other riders, other horses taking off, jumping in front, beside and behind you. This is a race where the fences, numbering ten at Burghley that day, all of steeplechasing pattern – even if one was constructed of plastic – and within the dimensions laid down for CC (Concours Complet International), have to be dealt with without the stimulus of flesh-and-blood competition. You race against the soulless, inevitable moment of the second hand on the timekeeper's watch, and while there are horses who will only work properly if they are galloped in company, others have to be trained for phase B on their own, in case on the day they refuse to go it alone.

Like most things, gauging the right speed for the steeplechase comes with experience, but roughly it equates to that at which a 2-mile hunt race at a point-to-point is run. At Burghley the distance, achieved by going twice round the course, was 3 kilometres 450 metres (2 miles 255 yards). The going can be misleading, trapping the most knowledgeable into pushing on where in fact it is unnecessary and merely takes more out of the horse than need be. Changes in the surface can also affect the horse's performance, as at Burghley where for part of the way the old turf is replaced by the hard, close-cropped fairway of the golf course. When the going on the cross-country promises to be heavy some competitors may choose deliberately to go steady on the steeplechase and incur time faults there, conserving their horses' strength for the rigours to come, but at the end of the day it is the best riders on the fittest horses that come within a few seconds of the correct time.

That day at Burghley only nine out of the thirty-one competitors who concluded all the phases of the event, incurred time faults on the steeplechase course, with Favour, Carawich, Benjie, and both Gretna Green and Brazil amongst those that went clear, and Richard Meade's young Tommy Buck only ·8 of a second outside the time.

Between phases C and D there is a ten-minute break, and during this time each horse is minutely inspected by a committee, comprising the official veterinary surgeon and two judges who have the responsibility of deciding whether the animal is fit to continue. Then comes the moment of all moments, the count-down to the start of the cross-country.

Much of the success of a three-day event from the point of view of the public rests with the weather, over which no-one has any control, and with the overall organization, which nowadays is usually exceptional. Both factors also influence the competitors' assessment of the event to a degree, but for them the chief onus lies fair and square on the shoulders of the course builder, the man who cannot please all the people all of the time.

In the past ten years or so, the cross-country courses, the heart of a three-day event, have become considerably more formidable, but with maximum heights and spreads of fences governed by stringent FEI rules, much of the difficulty of a course has to be determined by other means, and course designing and building is now recognized as a highly skilled art. Usually the aim is to include, and often strengthen, any natural obstacles such as Cotswold walls, that lend themselves to the general plan, linking these with an assortment of solidly constructed fences that present the rider with a variety of legitimate problems, plus a considerable ingredient of legitimate fright, but always with minimum risk to the horse. Fences have to be sited with due regard to the going, not only when they are built, which is normally in the previous winter, but bearing in mind the likely state of the ground when the course is used. The type of terrain and lie of the land, and the relation of the obstacles to each other are all important considerations affecting the severity of a fence and from which direction it should be approached. Usually about one third of the obstacles are spreads; water is used in various ways, and the combination fences and those with more than one way of being jumped are devised specifically to make the riders use their heads. Considerable ingenuity goes into designing a good variety of fences, and devising the materials from which they are constructed.

The Burghley Horse Trials were first held in 1961, substituting for the similar event that took place at Harewood from 1953 to 1959, and at first it was not certain whether there would be sufficient entries to keep going. Badminton was, and still is, *the* event of the year. It is held in the spring, once as the natural conclusion to the hunting season, and it was not altogether a popular idea to start up again with another season in the autumn. Burghley however did keep going to become a very popular fixture, sponsored by Raleigh Industries in the same way that Whitbreads support Badminton, and with a future doubly assured in 1969 when the Midland Bank extended its sponsorship to include almost all the official horse trials in the country.

The World Championships were held at Burghley in 1966 and 1974, and the European Championships in 1962 and 1971. In between these years the event is looked on as one with its own particular attractions and atmosphere, but without quite the prestige and demands of Badminton. Burghley is never a trial for the mediocre rider or horse. It is a splendid event to have in the background before tackling Badminton in the following April.

In the autumn of 1975 the picture was a little unusual. The weather had cancelled out Badminton, depriving the top competitors of their most valuable competitive experience, and the selectors of a most important yardstick for the coming Olympics. Unlike many of the other eventing nations, in Britain there is normally a wide choice of horses from which at least the initial selection of Olympic possibles could be made, but not always a comparable number of riders. Even amongst those at the top of the combined training tree, there are relatively few riders capable of giving a horse a very good dressage test and the same standards across country and in the show jumping arena, in a competition that amongst all the big events is, and has to be, that much bigger yet. Nor are the select handful who do come into this category necessarily partnered by comparable horses. In the totalitarian states they would be and the American system was devised to do the same, but in Britain the great horses as well as the lesser ones are almost exclusively privately owned. There is the magnanimous character who offers to loan a horse to the Olympic team, but the norm is for the eventing owner of a good horse, or the rider who has trained and brought it along himself, to want to ride it – and good luck to him or her! The selectors' task therefore is to choose the best possible combinations of horse and rider, and to do this they must not only go by the consistent placings of the past two seasons, they must see the candidates at a later date over a course sufficiently tough to be a genuine test.

The problem facing Colonel Nicoll, who had taken over from Bill Thomson, Burghley's previous cross-country architect, was the dual challenge of designing a course that fulfilled this purpose, without at the same time asking impossible questions of the type of competitor who normally makes a date with this event. Not all the fences were new. The Colonel had availed himself of some of the original expertise, and also left the first few to provide what they should, a straightforward introduction to bigger hazards to come. He then combined his own ingenuity to provide a real test that was fair, but sufficiently big and solid and problematical to sort out the men from the boys (and of course the girls from the little girls!), and to give some food for thought to those competitors who had arrived on the scene with more optimism than expertise.

Seen from the ground during those crucial policy-making walks round beforehand, the fences as usual looked enormous. Designed for goats! was Princess Anne's verdict, taking a knowledgeable and personally concerned interest in the course if, perforce, an academic one. It is something to be able to seek comfort from the truth, that the obstacles do look different when seen from the back of the horse, and it is a part of the vital mental approach to the sport to override, at least to an extent, the psychological effect of viewing fences from the disadvantageous position of one's own two feet. The object of the exercise of walking round is to note the going, to decide on tactics of speed and approach, to sum up the potential of each fence in turn, to test the depth of water in the Trout Hatchery if that seems an essential, and to walk the entire course usually twice over, as you mean to ride it. The thoroughness with which this is done and the experience and good sense employed in the preparation of riding a cross-country course are essential, and the things that can lessen or increase those stomach 'butterflies' as the hands of the starter's stop-watch come up to the point of no return.

John Kersley and Favour started, and it must have put heart into many

competitors waiting their turn to know how easy that attractive mare made
it all look, devouring the 6 kilometres 840 metres (4 miles 448 yards) course
with its twenty-nine fences within the 12 minute optimum time and without
penalty. But if that round was heartening to all, the pattern was soon
established. The better riders, most but not all with the better horses, went
round clear, and for them speed was the decisive factor, an average 20 mph
required to avoid time penalties. The less good were soon in varying degrees
of trouble before the day was out, and there were some performances to
catch, and many to cloud the eyes of the watching selectors.

And so hooves thudded over the ridge and furrow and the course clearers'
whistles blew, the crowds boosted good rounds and fine jumping with
clapping and encouragement, and struck fear into the breasts of already
anxious riders with audible gasps of horror when a horse took off too soon or
blundered. It was over the first, a post and rails, over the wooden wall, with
Lambert's Sofa causing no trouble either but some of the older horses not
altogether appreciating the hard going. That open ditch at No. 4 with its
different lines of approach might have looked a death-trap when viewed
from the ground, but if it did claim the odd victim, most went on to face the
first real bit of trouble, the Double Coffin. There it was not only Richard
Meade's young Tommy Buck that got the shock of his life as he jumped
down dubiously over the initial element to find himself faced with two
ditches at the bottom, before going on up and over the exit. Unfortunately
not all riders are possessed of Richard's notable drive and tact with a young
horse, the expertise that sent Tommy Buck leaping across the ditches, despite
his doubts, and then to start giving thought to what he was about.

All cross-country courses seem to develop a 'bogy' of some sort as the day
wears on, sometimes a fence that appears relatively innocuous on the walk
round but then claims a victim and suddenly starts to take its toll, often
initially in the minds of riders yet to come. At Burghley most of the trouble
occurred at the big Trakener, heavy poles set in a ditch in a depression that
made for a sloping-down approach, a fence that looked as nasty as it proved
for the many who had not the nerve to set sail at it and gallop on. The crowds
always jostle for position at places like the Trout Hatchery where good,
spectacular fun is provided for those who do not happen to be the ones
engendering it, and they were not disappointed. There was a worrying
moment for Richard when Tommy Buck forgot his hind legs and had to
slither them over the jump-in in pursuit of his front ones, only to jump out
with a will and go on his way with increasing confidence. There was a worse
moment for Mark Phillips when Gretna Green blundered on landing in the

water, and only the seat of a limpet saved him from a ducking. Aly Pattinson with Olivia, her first ride that day, really gave the spectators their money's worth by diving in head first, but she was not the only one to need a change of clothing, and some competitors went out there, after their horses had viewed the whole watery complex with irrevocable distaste from the wrong side.

Mark's first horse, Brazil, had the disastrous notion of banking the big Birch Fence at No. 11, but withdrew a front leg just in time. For some riders the psychological effect of jumping up a slope into the darkness of a wood, overshadowed the fact that the fence was a small problem for their horses, others chose the wrong route for their particular animals up the bank to the Zig-Zag Wall at the Dairy Farm. The size and spread of the parallel rails looked just as formidable as they were, and after them there was only a fence to go before the big question mark of the course, the Maze.

It was a combination of cut and laid fences varying in height between 3 feet 6 inches and 3 feet 10 inches, and presented several routes. The shorter but more difficult one over the left-hand corner offered an advantage in time and distance, but demanded a very bold and athletic horse. Of the three who tried it, one rider took a painful but fortunately undamaging purler that did not prevent her from remounting to continue. The other two reaped the benefit of their courage to complete the course and finish in twenty-first and twenty-second in the final placings. Surprisingly, in all there were only two falls and two refusals at this unusual obstacle, though some horses tried to bank it and Mark had the luck with him when Gretna Green put her feet on it.

With the Maze behind them the remaining ten fences seemed comparatively straightforward, with time the main bugbear, and an oddity or two, like the fence built of upright tree stumps to enliven them. As the day wore on there were more polished rounds by the experienced partnerships, there were tired horses and horses not so fit, and a few who should not have been there at all. There were hard luck stories, and stories of genuine bad luck for some and good luck for others. There were falls and close shaves, some brilliant riding, some not so good, plenty of sheer guts and courage, and a number of shapely bottoms seen to advantage in the stretch breeches of the predominating female competitors. For the thirty-five per cent who were eliminated or retired there was still the satisfaction of having been there and had a go, for the remaining riders there was the wonderful sight of the big tree trunks on the Raleigh wagon that comprised the last fence. And as the last competitor on the course there was Aly Pattinson with the seven-year-old Carawich, to dash some of the hopes of the leaders, complete a round that capped Favour's in making it all look easy, and shoot her and her horse up into the lead.

On the last day thirty-one horses, out of the original forty-eight that began the event, survived the morning's veterinary inspection, to arrive eventually in the collecting ring for the final phase. It was an admirable jumping course that belied its easy appearance, especially for horses that on the previous day had covered a total of nearly 14 miles and jumped thirty-nine obstacles.

With the order of the placed runners reversed tension soon started to build up, and as the leading riders began their rounds with scores sufficiently close to keep the competition wide open, the excitement began spiralling to fever pitch.

In this phase each knock down, and the first disobedience in the whole test, exacts 10 penalties, the second disobedience 20, the third elimination, and there is a 30 point penalty for fall of horse and/or rider. In the earlier stages someone knocked up a cricket score of 100, and only eleven riders, with only three of those in the final dozen, went clear. John Kersley with Favour was one, consolidating the good efforts of the mare's cross-country to come up a place to fourth. When Tommy Buck just tipped the gate, that allowed Mark and Gretna Green to pip Richard for second place, which must have cheered Janet Hodgson, confined by her injuries at Luhmuhlen to watching her black mare's prowess on television.

Aly Pattinson and Carawich were once more last to go. It takes nerve and a cool head and fine riding to give a horse the best chance when the pressures are on, and so much at stake, and Aly gave him the lot while tension mounted until it was almost tangible and the crowds held their breath. They made one mistake at the last combination, but they could afford to, and Aly Pattinson and Carawich, competing in their first big three-day event, won the Raleigh Trophy by 6·86 points from Mark Phillips, competing with Gretna Green, one of his last-minute rides.

That was an exciting and significant Burghley in the autumn of 1975. In April 1976 there was what promised to be a truly vintage Badminton to cap it.

It all began when the 1948 Olympic Games were held in England, and as Vice-President of the FEI the Duke of Beaufort went to watch the first-ever combined training event to be held in this country. The British team made laudable efforts but was eliminated, but the Duke was an immediate convert to a sport that seemed, with the possible exception of the dressage phase, tailor-made for the national qualities of British riders and horses, and promptly offered the British Horse Society his Gloucestershire estate as a venue for a three-day event.

Conceived principally as a training ground for pre-Olympic competing, and organized in April to comply with farming and hunting commitments, the first Badminton Horse Trials were held in 1949. The cross-country course was built to suit the ability of one of the Duke's best hunters that tested the fences as they went up – if the horse jumped it, the obstacle was left in, if he did not it was amended until he complied. One combination, christened the Coffin from the shape of the sunken ditch that is an integral part of it, has been included in the course almost every year since, and is still liable to cause as much trouble as in the year of its inception.

The competitors had to be British subjects over the age of seventeen, their horses 15 h.h. or over, and not more than ten years old – an age now considered to be the peak of an eventer's life, with some of the best still going strong at thirteen and even older. Oddly, since women were then excluded from the Olympics, the competition, to be held annually for three years, was open to them, but advertised as having the sole aim of finding riders and horses suitable as training for a team to compete in the 1952 Olympics in Helsinki. But obviously the lady riders were not taken very seriously because a special prize was offered to any who completed the course. Of the five who started only one did finish, but she upset the form by coming fifth overall, and so paving the way for Sheila Willcox, as yet the only rider to achieve the hat-trick at Badminton, and all the gallant girls who now gallop the event courses of the world with such marked success.

There were seventy starters for Badminton in 1976. In 1949 twenty-two competitors set out to blaze the trail in this new British sport, riding in the wet weather and deep going that are only too typical of this event. On the cross-country they had the fun of choosing their own line, which must have added to the excitements of the surprisingly large number of spectators who attended over the three days, and many of whom were straggling round the long, elongated course that was only compressed into a more circular route for their convenience, some years later.

Some of those who entered had decided they were 'overfaced' when walking round the cross-country and promptly withdrew from the competition, a number more failed to make the grade either there or previously on the steeplechase, and one horse was retired on the final morning. In the end twelve came in to jump, and only the horse that came second achieved a clear round. The winner was the American bred and owned Golden Willow, that was broken and schooled in Middleburgh, trained in England as a five-year-old at the well-known Cotswold Equitation School at Kingham, and ridden to victory by the school's proprietor, the noted horseman, John Shedden.

That first Badminton aroused interest amongst a section of British horsemen other than the already converted, although there were still plenty to damn the dressage test as so much 'circus nonsense'. Nevertheless there were forty-five entries the next year to brave a lengthened speed and endurance phase with seven extra fences. Eighteen horses finished, and the gate was trebled.

By 1951 the competition had been opened to foreign riders. In the following year the presence of the Queen and her family ensured the event's success from the attendance point of view, and gave the royal visitors the first of those happy, informal days out with the horses at Badminton that they have been enjoying nearly every year since. In 1953 the newly devised European Championships were staged at Badminton, six years later freak weather produced appalling conditions for competitors and spectators alike, and for the Duke a devastating churned-up sea of mud disfiguring his beautiful park. Again on account of the weather the 1963 trials were run as a one-day event, and were cancelled altogether by threatened or actual worse conditions in 1963, 1966, and 1975.

Badminton form can be unpredictable and has produced a few one-time-only winners. Equally many great names, of riders and horses, have been made initially at this most popular of three-day events. Lieutenant-Colonel Weldon, an Olympic competitor, who took over as Badminton course designer in 1956 and became Director of the trials two years later, as a major in command of the King's Troop RHA, consolidated his famous career with the great Kilbarry by winning in 1956. Two out of Sheila Willcox's three consecutive Badminton victories were with High and Mighty, by a thoroughbred out of a Highland Pony crossed with an Arabian mare, that used his pony blood cleverness to clear fences with minimum effort, either just folding his legs up out of the way or scrambling up one side of an obstacle and down the other. 1960 and 1961 were the years of the great Australian riders, Bill Roycroft with Our Solo, and Laurie Morgan with Salad Days, and it was Ireland's turn in 1965 when Major Boylan rode Durlas Eile into first place. All three winning horses, in 1964 (Captain Templar on M'Lord Connolly), 1967 (Miss Ross Taylor's Johnathan), and 1969 (Richard Walker's Pasha), were Anglo-Arabs. Jane Bullen's Our Nobby, winner in 1968, was pony-sized.

In 1971 Mark Phillips won with Great Ovation, with Princess Anne and

Doublet fifth in their first three-day event. The next year Mark and Ovation repeated the effort, just pipping on the post Richard Meade and The Poacher, the winners in 1970. Lucinda Prior-Palmer with Be Fair galloped and jumped impressively to the fore in 1973. The following year was when Mark took the Whitbread Trophy for the third time, to prove just what a horse Columbus could be.

Since its inception there have been notable Badmintons and others slightly less memorable, there have been a great many falls but remarkably few accidents in a sport that by its very nature must contain an element of danger, and the seasonal severity of the course has increased or diminished a little in relation to the proximity of the Olympic Games. What has built up through the years is the undeniable prestige attached to riding in, let alone winning horse trials that are unique in the world of combined training.

From 7 to 10 April inclusive 1976, comprised the twenty-fifth anniversary of the Badminton Horse Trials, their Silver Jubilee year taking place only four months before the Olympics in Montreal. It was all set to be a vintage event. The sun shone all the time, the crowds were an all-time record, the going promised to be fast and proved to be near perfect. The cross-country was testing, the problems principally arising with the tricky relationship of one fence to another, and the additional effort of coping with a series of combination jumps after the supreme trial of the water. The verdict on the course, both before and after riding it, was very tough but fair.

Four girls were holding the first four places after the dressage phase, where riders in top hats and swallow-tail coats, with one or two in uniform, riding shining, perfectly plaited and turned-out horses, endeavoured to match performance to the elegance of their appearance. Heading the list was Janet Hodgson, with the veteran Larkspur reaffirming his worth before retiring to the hunting field he loves, with Aly Pattinson and Olivia second, Lucinda Prior-Palmer and Wideawake third, Miranda Frank with Touch and Go fourth. Mark Phillips was fifth with Brazil and seventh with Favour, with his Persian Holiday, ridden *hors concours*, producing a more attractive and better marked test than either.

By early Saturday morning tens of thousands of cars were converging on Badminton, and as the later arrivals were being slotted into the car-parks the first competitors were setting off on the preliminary three miles plus of roads and tracks, with two miles of steeplechase to come, followed by a further six miles plus of tracks before the start of the cross-country. Two horses were withdrawn before starting the second day, two after phase B, four after the steeplechase, where the required speed called for an average of 26 mph to avoid penalty. The sun still shone. There were thirty-five fences to negotiate across country, seven miles to go. The Queen, the Queen Mother, Prince Philip and other members of the family at intervals dashed around in a Landrover to different fences, where strategically placed farm wagons allowed them to stand and see over the heads of the crowds. Prince Charles, sporting a full and conveniently concealing naval beard, borrowed a horse and rode to his vantage points in the company of Sir John Miller, the Crown Equerry. Princess Anne, wishing she was competing, helped Mark with his horses, and when the time came peered anxiously into a TV set so that she could follow his progress on his three separate rounds.

Mark, first to go, looked lean, pared down to the last possible ounce and with around thirty-three miles in the saddle already behind him, set off with Brazil. It was not a very happy experience. Maybe the big horse was just having an off day, maybe losing a shoe at No. 3, the Pardubice Taxis, made him uncomfortably foot-sore, or maybe he fancied the big stuff less than he thought he would. He took one of the expected bogies, the Chevrons, three sets of rails with several routes, in copybook style, but had propped at one fence before trying it again as Mark really drove him over the Pardubice Snake Fence, and then pecked on landing.

The Lake was more difficult than ever before. As he came into the approach Brazil was making it plain he was not keen about jumping the 3 foot high tree trunks on the jetty, with a nasty little one on top to stop a horse banking it and a steep drop down into the water. Compelled by strong riding the horse landed unbalanced and pecked again, then with all impulsion gone held unwillingly to the 4 foot log lying in 2 feet of water, he half scrambled over to fall flat the other side.

Mark had a taste of that Lake before, when Columbus dunked him in it in 1973, but he philosophically lay on his back on the bank, legs in the air to empty his boots, and then continued on his way. They went very steadily but coped well with the Normandy Bank and the tricky drops of the Double Ski Jump, before galloping on up and over the Faggot Pile at No. 22.

There was nothing much about the next, the combination of the Sunken Road, to worry a horse of this calibre, but Brazil had had enough. After the second refusal Mark wisely retired him, and rode off contemplating the answer to one of four questions, concerning which one of his four 'possible' horses might make it to the Olympic short-list.

Then the girls started taking over. There was the experienced trooper, Barbara Hammond, who used to ride the equally experienced Eagle Rock, sailing over the first assortment of fences with the big Red Rusky, over the

Bullfinch and Beechers, making nothing of the Giant's Table or the Lake, or of the big star and equally big Cirencester Rails, enjoying the course but clocking up a lot of time faults. There were Jane Starkey and Topper Too going bounce! bounce! bounce! plumb across the centre of the Chevrons on their way to a clear, but still not within the optimum time. Janet Hodgson, bent on giving Larkspur back his confidence after calamities in Germany, went clear too, but slowly, then later had another clear with Gretna Green, with the mare, beautifully balanced, popping neatly down into the Lake and over the log with no trouble at all.

Sadly, after her Burghley triumph, it was not Aly Pattinson's day. Olivia had put on her usual attractive exhibition in the dressage arena and was dealing competently with the fences until she jumped in too big at the Chevrons, stopped, and as she was whisked round to take an alternative route, overstepped the tight penalty zone. Later, with the Trout Hatchery at Burghley in mind, Aly stoked up the little ex-show hack and Foxhunter jumper and came in fast to the lake, but again the pair provided the crowd with one of the excitements of the day as the mare tried, but failed to bank the logs and her rider nose-dived into the water. Olivia scrambled up out of reach and, while Aly fumbled in the depths for her whip, took off on what must have been a most refreshing swim. Reunited eventually, the pair finished the course, but that was not the end of the road for Aly. Carawich, her chief hope, had been unsettled in the dressage by the general excitement. On the cross-country he stopped at the Chevrons, and then fell heavily at the combination of crossed rails called the Star. Despite an injured hand, his rider remounted, and the pair showed their mettle by continuing to the end.

Out of the first twenty-seven to go seven were retired or eliminated. By quarter-time Hugh Thomas was in the lead with Playamar, a grand type of big galloping horse, active and clever with it, that was third with Hugh in the World Championships and then dropped out of the 1974 season with tendon trouble. Topper Too was lying second, Red Rusky third, Gretna Green fourth.

Some of the smaller horses, like Vincent Jones's Bleak Hills, set off on what looked to be a very short-lived effort, but after a slow and adventurous start that piled up the penalties with the bigger fences, showed a cat-like competence in dealing with the formidable drops and those needing clever, precise jumping, like the newly designed Quarry. There were several horses to come to the top of the rise before fence No. 5 and show a marked dislike of the view. Three ended up in the ditch, and Jane Holderness-Roddam's Triojoy was extricated with some difficulty from under the Zig-Zag Rails.

At one stage Charlotte Steel and Gamble were second, Topper Too dropped back to third, Virginia Thompson fourth with Cornish Duke. Hugh Thomas and Playamar were still first, with the commanding lead they retained until Mark Phillips set out on his second round, this time with the grey Favour, jumping neatly, bouncing down the centre of the Chevrons, and going a good gallop to finish only $1\frac{1}{2}$ time faults behind. By the time Richard Meade and the big Jacob Jones lined up the order was Playamar, Favour, the fast fourteen-year-old Touch and Go, Gamble, Topper Too.

When it really matters there is no event rider in the world more capable of pulling out the stops than Richard Meade. And Badminton 1976 did matter, his best horse, Tommy Buck, was lame, and the eight-year-old, 17 h.h. Jacob Jones was the triple gold medallist's only hope for a ticket to Montreal. Perhaps because of his size the horse had matured slowly and for all his promise was slow in coming to the game, but Richard's unhurried, meticulous preparation was to pay off. There were one or two fences where his outstanding mixture of drive and coaxing, so essential with an inexperienced horse, was more apparent than others: they were a little close to the first contention in Luckington Lane and there was an anxious moment amongst the trees in Huntsman's Close, but they went a gallop that brought them within ·93 seconds of Favour, and 1·53 of Playamar. It was an impressive performance that should have gladdened the hearts of the selectors.

Somewhere near the end Mark brought out Persian Holiday to cap his good dressage test with a good steady round that included only one stop, in the Lake where for a fraught second the water once more must have looked very wet. To finish the day came Lucinda Prior-Palmer with Wideawake.

The horse, at ten the perfect age for an eventer, looked a picture, athletic, beautifully balanced, going a great gallop yet always within himself, ears pricked as he sailed on confidently to his fences. In the dressage arena Lucinda had calmed Wideawake's normal impetuousness to give them the best mark in the test, on the cross-country the pair illustrated for all to see just what a real partnership between rider and horse can achieve. Lucinda is completely attuned to her horses, an economical rider who takes the shortest route, wastes neither time nor energy, and obtains the maximum out of her horse without ever pushing it. Their mutual confidence was as apparent as their mutual enjoyment, and this is a rider as quick to slip the reins at moments like the one when Wideawake put in a short stride going into the Lake, as she was to give him an encouraging pat as he galloped on up the hill after completing the complex as well as any horse that day. There were no mistakes, it was the second fastest round, and a brilliant, masterly performance that tipped them into the lead with points to spare.

There had been plenty of drama during the day, although in the end no more than the average number of refusals and withdrawals, with more of the last occurring after the steeplechase than usual. There was a tragedy for Sue Hatherly when twelve-year-old Harley, ex-reserve horse for the Australian team at Munich, broke down at the penultimate fence and was found to have snapped a tendon. Of the Irish contingent, hoping for placings that would allow two of them to fill the vacancies in the Irish Olympic team, Thunder ran out of steam in the Lake. But both Clonrochem, piloted by Brian Mullins, and Blue Tom Tit, ridden by his intrepid owner, Van de Vater, went clear but with time faults to finalize the event in fourteenth and twenty-fourth places. There was Second Lieutenant Wathen out to get round Badminton with Island Monarch come what may, somewhat literally smiting the course hip and thigh at intervals, up to and including the Hayrack at No. 34, but still making it through the Whitbread Bar for home. The spectacular drops at the Normandy Bank and the Double Ski Jump kept the crowds in suspense and worried the riders, but provided surprisingly little trouble for the horses. The four separate leaps at the Sunken Road caught out those without the boldness or agility to achieve them, the Chevrons attracted a crowd all day, fascinated by the efforts of riders, some successful, some not, to choose the right way for their particular horse. Michael Tucker and the big Ben Wyvis had to have a second think here, Chris Collins's Smokey VI did the same, but later on the course made a daring and accurate leap across the centre of the Star at No. 28, and made the fastest time, but owing partly to inattention during the dressage, finally came tenth.

Not even Smokey managed the course in the optimum time of 11 minutes 28 seconds, and in a way it seemed strange that no-one availed themselves of the stretches of perfect going to save time penalties, but it was early in the season and riders were understandably cautious with their horses' legs. They were also treating the big, beautifully constructed fences with the respect they deserved.

There were thirty-eight out of the original seventy entries to jump in the arena on the final day. The sun still shone, the stands were packed to capacity, the royal family were there in force, the Queen to present the trophy, Princess Anne with Goodwill, brought along to take a look at the proceedings. By the afternoon the tail had been dealt with and it was coming up to the stars, Lucinda in a commanding position, those in second, third and fourth places all very close with 10 penalty points covering the lot. It was a gay scene staging a really exciting finish. It was a real vintage Badminton.

The course had one change of rein, was spacious and straightforward but still posed questions for riders and horses coming to it after the rigorous efforts of the day before. Only Carawich and Bo'sun were clear when Clarissa Strachan and Merry Sovereign came in to jump. They had one fence down for 10 penalties and a final placing of fifth. Richard Meade came in, lying fourth, the atmosphere electric. He took it steadily, but clear and within the optimum time. Favour followed, rapping a couple but like Jacob Jones stepping well out over the water. As they approached the last fence maybe Mark gave a fleeting thought to Burghley 1973, when he and Maid Marion demolished the ultimate one. Fortunately they still had enough in hand to win, and this time there was no mistake. A clear round, and third place, at least, consolidated. Hugh Thomas could not afford to have one down, but Playamar, jumping big and boldly gave him no qualms to keep them second.

With a 12·8 lead over these two Lucinda and Wideawake had little to fear, even if in the past the show jumping had not always been the horse's most reliable phase. But Wideawake was enjoying himself, looking as fit and well as though the 14 miles of the previous day's speed and endurance had never existed, and a perfect clear round did credit to the good work his rider had put in with him in the preceding weeks.

And so they won, for Lucinda fulfilling twice over the dream of every event rider to win at Badminton, for Wideawake the proof that here was a marvellous second string to her potential Olympic horse, Be Fair.

It was a popular and well-deserved victory and the applause was thunderous as they rode in to receive the Whitbread Trophy from the Queen. As Lucinda turned Wideawake to canter their lap of honour the horse reared, staggered, collapsed and died.

This was an appalling tragedy, made worse by happening where and when it did, but the demands of the three-day trials at Badminton were not the cause. As with every horse that competes in a three-day event, Wideawake had been subjected to three stringent veterinary examinations, before the start of the dressage, at the end of the steeplechase, and on the final morning before the jumping phase. And no horse came into the arena that day looking fitter or more full of *joie de vivre* than Lucinda Prior-Palmer's bay. In the past, through ignorance and inexperience a number of horses were entered for three-day events without the essential physical fitness, but this seldom happens today and would never be the case with riders of

Lucinda's calibre, who pay meticulous attention to the long, careful preparation of their horses, and train them to a hair for what they are expected to do.

It is now thought that Wideawake's death was caused by a severe nervous spasm of the vagal nerve, which controls some actions of the larynx, heart and lungs. This can occur under an anaesthetic or very occasionally when a horse is in a highly excited state just after light exercise. For a horse as fit as Wideawake the showjumping phase provided this condition, especially as a high-powered horse always reacts to crowds, atmosphere, having done well, and having been praised for it.

That the disaster happened in front of the Queen and thousands of spectators made it harder to bear, but nevertheless was incidental to what is fortunately the rarest of happenings and quite unconnected with the type of competition.

All sports call for mental disciplines by those who compete, to cope with the disappointments and calamities that do occur from time to time, and combined training is no exception to the rule. When Captain Malcolm Wallace, competing in the 1975 Midland Bank Horse Trials Championships with Eastern Promise, had completed a fast, clear round after a good dressage test, it was discovered that the timing apparatus had broken down, and there was no recourse but to ignore his cross-country score and eliminate him. As he would certainly have been placed and might even have won, Captain Wallace's unequivocal acceptance of what must have been a bitter disappointment, was in the character of the true sportsman.

The moment when her Olympic horse, Cornish Gold, got hung up on the notorious Coffin fence at Badminton, Bridget Parker needed all her self discipline to keep her cool and stop the animal from panicking. After jumping in over the rail Goldie had checked slightly at sight of the ditch in the bottom and indulged his occasional habit of kicking back, to come to a grinding halt with his hock over the top of the rail, and the leg wound back through the one below. The only hope was to prevent the horse from struggling, and since he could be difficult to control from the ground, Bridget stayed where she was in the saddle, talking to him, soothing him, doing everything she knew to keep him quiet, and praying they would be quick in cutting down the fence. After what seemed like hours but was in fact only a minute or so, her level-headed action saved Cornish Gold from any injury and the pair went straight on to complete the course. And this presented the Combined Training Committee, and the fence judge with a problem. The horse had not refused in the first instance because his front legs were over the fence, neither horse nor rider could be said to have fallen because Bridget had not dismounted, and the moment he was free Goldie went on through, so how to penalize the competitor? In the end Bridget was given time faults only, but because of this incident the Grand Jury later changed the FEI rules.

Compared with the tragedy of Wideawake these incidents pale to insignificance, but it is to be hoped that never again will anyone be called on to display fortitude in face of the million to one chance that in her hour of victory robbed Lucinda Prior-Palmer, not just of a brilliant performer with a potentially brilliant future, but of the dear companion of her days.

For all that happened afterwards, those who saw the winning pair at Badminton 1976 were treated to a display of superb horsemanship and understanding between horse and rider. For all that clouded the concluding moments, Badminton through the days retained its magic.

And since one of the functions of the main trials was to help the Olympic team selectors in their task, the results made that problem easier by producing a tailor-made short list of 'probables'. Both Goodwill and Be Fair and their riders were excused Badminton on their past showing, and though Princess Anne was later injured in a fall, that did not impair her chances. The placings at Badminton then added Mark Phillips with Favour, and Persian Holiday on his *hors concours* performance, Richard Meade with Jacob Jones, and Hugh Thomas with Playamar. For playing safe there was now also a supplementary list of 'possibles', including Clarissa Strachan with Merry Sovereign, Chris Collins with Smokey, Diana Thorne with the Kingmaker, a well-known speed combination that despite a fall finished thirteenth, and Michael Tucker with Ben Wyvis, twenty-sixth at Badminton, and in 1975, seventh in the European Championships and placed at Ledyard Farm in America.

The final team for Montreal consisted of the above short list of probables, with Mark Phillips as reserve.

All four completed the gruelling cross-country, with Richard Meade fourth in the final individual placings, and Princess Anne twenty-fourth after a heavy fall at fence nineteen. But Be Fair's tendon slipped at the end of a brilliant round, and Playamar's subsequent lameness eliminated the team. Ill luck and boggy going put paid to Britain's former dominance.

6

To win at Badminton is every event rider's dream, to get round the cross-country is a part of the vision, just to compete fulfils the ambitions of the majority. At Badminton 1976 one of the main functions was to find potentials for the Olympic team, but another annual objective, and one of increasing importance, is to give the competitors some idea of what to expect if they ever do get the chance of competing abroad in an international event.

In America and Australia, as in England, combined training is a comparatively young sport, but if not quite in its present form eventing has been popular on the Continent for many years, and a three-day event was included in the 1912 Olympic Games.

Combined Training has its roots in the French cavalry schools where it was called the *militaire*, a name that is sometimes still used. This was a three-day test designed to prove the efficiency or otherwise of the specialized training given to the horses, to make them as effective as possible in war. The riders had to demonstrate their animals' obedience and handiness in a phase approximating to the dressage test, and then their courage and endurance in tackling various hazards over many miles of different and often the roughest types of terrain. The horses' state of physical fitness was gauged by their ability to meet more demands on the third day, after only a short period of rest. The high degree of training ensured the riders being as bold and fit as their horses, and with horsemanship, judgement, and a sympathetic co-operation with their animals to match.

Today the select little band of officers and non-commissioned officers who comprise the famous *Cadre Noir* include competing in horse trials amongst their superb all-round horsemanship, and the corps instructs military and civilian riders in eventing as well as other competitive forms of equitation.

When the *militaire* developed into the *concours complet* of today some of the big state studs provided perfect settings for France's annual events, and in 1973 the Junior European Championships were held at the Pompadour Stud in Limousin. Another celebrated venue is Haras du Pin, dating from 1338 the oldest known royal stud in Normandy and once the personal property of King Philippe VI. No doubt the fifty-six horses he kept there showed the characteristics most prized in medieval equines – and possibly in some jet-age ones as well. They consisted of:

Three qualities of the fox . . . short, straight ears, a good coat, a bushy tail; four of the hare . . . a narrow head, alertness, light movement and quick going; two of the ox . . . wide hindquarters, large eyes protruding from the head; three of the donkey . . . good feet, strong spine, and gentle nature; and of the Virgin, four . . . beautiful mane, beautiful breast, beautiful loins and fat buttocks.

The lovely facilities of the Le Pin Estate include hills and valleys, and hundreds of hectares of wood and pasture with intersecting bridle paths that could be utilized when the French organized the European Championships there in 1969.

In 1974 the French Council of Equitation sent a welcome invitation to the British Horse Society, for riders to come over and compete in the annual French Championships. On inquiry the standard of the competition was said to be mid-way between the Tidworth and Burghley events, and four suitable horses with their delighted young riders were duly dispatched.

Like the hospitality received at Haras du Pin the beauty of the environment exceeded expectations, but it was a little nonplussing to discover the assessment of the standard of the competition considerably lower than the reality. The steeplechase, held on the race track, was a big course designed in a bewildering figure of eight. The pattern of the cross-country, virtually the same course as that used for the European Championships, was set by the second fence, a maximum-height-and-spread parallel, met at the top of a large mound that was itself approached down a steep dip.

Only six horses went clear out of the fifteen that completed the course, but despite their qualms this included two of the British contingent. Angela Tucker had one stop with Moon Coin to come tenth, and Virginia Holgate and Jason went clear. Despite a fence down in the jumping phase, Virginia then had the thrill of gradually notching up from fifth to second place.

The next year six riders from Italy and five from England were among the thirty-two competitors who set out to enjoy the hospitality of their French hosts, and to tackle the big fences at Haras du Pin, this time with the added hazard of shocking weather conditions. With the sand dressage arena under water this phase took place in a covered school, where the British riders acquitted themselves creditably and were complimented on their neat turn-out and standard of riding. The difficulties of the cross-country, very well built and much the same as before, were increased by the heavy going in a country of big ditches and bigger banks, and in the muddy conditions the optimum time appeared unattainable. Only thirteen from thirty-two starters finished the second day, but with four British riders in the first ten. The fifth, Virginia Holgate, this time with her gallant little Dubonnet, went clear to fence 16 where the horse slipped at a rail on to a bank, landed on his stomach and was bruised and winded. Diana Thorne and the Kingmaker went a magnificent gallop to finish clear in the fastest time on both steeplechase and cross-country courses, and won the event with points to spare. As a focus for Badminton 1976, Jane Starkey and Topper Too were fourth, Miranda Frank with Touch and Go, sixth.

Until bulk precluded it Henry VIII showed some interest in *manège* riding, but even when the Renaissance brought new concepts of horsemanship and a new understanding of the mentality of the horse to supercede the brutal methods of older times, in England there was little of the Continental appreciation of equitation as an art. Elegant horsemanship might be a requisite of the European nobility, but with the exception of the Duke of Newcastle (1592–1676), in England the blue-blooded spent more time in the country hunting and racing than at court, whereas on the Continent *manège* riding was the vogue. The European princes and nobles might flock to the famous Neapolitan Riding School in Italy, foreigners might learn fine horsemanship there in order to instruct on their home ground, there might be slight differences between the French and German schools they founded, but the English were indifferent. Once fox-hunting was established as a national sport, except for what was preserved in the army riding schools, any form of an English school of horsemanship vanished.

This is not to suggest that English riders and horses were not good at going across country, in this field of sport they were unsurpassed, but horses were a means of conveyance for pursuing the art of hunting with hounds, and there was little conscious use of horsemanship, or schooling horses, or of the 'aids'. In Europe the picture remained a different one. While the British continued to spend their winters in happily chasing the fox, their months of early spring in racing, the Europeans were forced by the continental climate to concentrate on *manège* riding, the art of dressage, and eventually jumping in covered schools. While the Europeans for centuries bred horses that were comfortable in their paces, the English bred animals supreme in the world for galloping and jumping.

When eventing first arrived in England, the British got over their prejudice of dressage as best they could, trusting to their type of riding and horse to be able to pick up the necessary points by going flat-out across country. The Europeans excelled in the dressage phase, but were at a disadvantage across country, particularly in spring events as their harsh winters made it impossible for them to have their horses fit and trained as early in the year as the English animals.

For this reason the European Championships have not been held at Badminton again since the year of their inception in 1953, although a Swiss, Captain Schwarzenbach, riding Vae Victis, won the horse trials there two years previously. In 1954 the Championships were staged at Basle and the British and German teams were the only two to finish.

The Swedes won the 1957 European Championships at Copenhagen, and the early Olympic events were dominated by their riders. They are dressage-minded as a nation, and the internationally famous riding horse breed, the Swedish Halfbred, has action and temperament well-suited to dressage and combined training.

Each year an increasing number of British riders compete in the three-day events that are held in many European countries, and wherever they go are assured of wonderful hospitality, excellent sport and usually a heartening measure of success.

Recognition of the vital role played by the course builder has now led to international conventions on the subject. In time this must produce some sort of uniformity in steeplechase and cross-country courses, regardless of which country is staging the event. In some ways this would be a pity and could detract from the fun and interest of competing abroad, where local conditions, fence materials and ideas add an edge to the day. On the other hand more common knowledge on how to design courses and build jumps would do away with fences like those encountered, on one occasion only at Punchestown, when the World Championships of 1970 were held in Ireland, on the site that is famous for producing one of the toughest, but normally most highly regarded three-day events of the season. And though an unusually large number of eliminations on the cross-country often means that a large number of competitors were insufficiently skilful, it can occur because the course was too difficult for the standard of the competition. This was the case in the 1974 European Junior Championships in Rome, when the bulk of the competitors were unable to cope with the cross-country, and is something that international know-how would help to remedy in the future.

When British riders competed in Bavaria's third international event held on the Achselschwang State Farm, they found the entertainment organized for each evening matched up to the excellent test provided by the cross-country, and the first-class accommodation prepared for riders and horses alike.

Typical German thoroughness and efficiency are well suited to running combined training competitions, a sport that is annually growing more popular with the German nation, and it has been said that the equestrian set-up offered at the Munich Olympics in 1972 surpassed any in the world. The stabling, with push-button doors, air conditioning, special horse showers and central passages with anti-slip flooring, was in individual blocks housing a minimum of twenty horses, according to nationality and overlooked by comparable accommodation for their grooms. There was a blacksmith's and a saddler's shop, and a vast and impressive covered school, cool and quiet on even the hottest day, was supplemented by a circular wooden building for lungeing, and a sandpit for exercising in the same way outside. The main schooling area comprised two sand rings, and another enormous grass arena complete with schooling banks and various movable fences, with a mile-long sand track for galloping outside the perimeter. As a future centre of instruction at regional, national or international level this was a complex that could scarcely be bettered.

There were teams and individual competitors from Britain, Canada, Australia, Ireland and the USA. They came from Italy, Sweden, East Germany, Switzerland and France, from Holland, Poland, Austria, Hungary and Bulgaria, from the Argentine, Mexico, and the USSR. With the host nation, nineteen different nationalities and many different breeds of horse came before the panel of eminent judges during the two days of dressage.

The enormous stadium seating 28,000, like the other stands round the arena was packed to capacity on both days, a tribute to a form of equitation well understood and popular with a nation whose riders practise the art all through winter, and with whom instructing dressage is a prized occupation. And because of this outlook, one not generally applicable in Britain, and because in Germany dressage is taught as the basis of all horsemanship, that huge crowd of spectators appreciated exactly what was going on and derived an absorbing interest from seeing the displays of equitation.

Mary Gordon-Watson and Cornishman, first of the British team to go, put Britain into the lead for a while, and by the end of the day was seventh place, only 13 points behind the leader, the Swiss, Max Hauri riding an Irish horse. Bridget Parker and Cornish Gold were in contention, and on the second day Mark Phillips's test bumped Britain back into fourth position, and provided an interesting contrast to Richard Meade's.

Great Ovation's performance was accurate, obedient and smooth, and very pleasing to the eye if a little lacking in impulsion.

Richard was riding the Allhusens' home-bred Laurieston, a horse with a good temperament but a strong animal, one that needs knowing both in the dressage arena and going across country. On that important day Laurieston was as fit as it is possible to get any horse, and he was inattentive and potentially explosive. Richard felt as though he was sitting on a volcano and was praying they would not jump out of the arena, but by a judicious mixture of kidding the horse along and the quiet tact for which his riding is well known, he managed to keep things under control. Despite transitions that were noticeably rough and jerky, luck and maybe some lenient markings were with him, and they finished the test with a creditable mark of 50·67.

The European Championships, organized every two years in the uneven date years between the Olympic Games, are one thing, the World Championships, held every four years in the even date between them, are another. But the three-day event at the Olympics is, and has to be something apart, something extra. This is the test of all tests, the Grand National of the eventing world, devised for the cream of the horsemen and horses that have been selected on performance over a long period and after stringent tests and arduous training. It has to provide the stiffest, most exacting trial possible without unduly hazarding the horses, and the speed and endurance phase at Munich fulfilled all the obligations.

At the end of the dressage phase a West German riding a big Hanovarian was in the lead, Bill Roycroft, the indomitable fifty-seven-year-old captain of the Australian team, lying second. In all seventy-three riders lined up in turn for the start of the first assignment of roads and tracks, fifty were still in the running by the end of the day, there were no serious accidents and not one horse was permanently damaged.

The cross-country course was in keeping with the exceptionally high standards maintained throughout. The fences were imposing, massive, many constructed with natural spruce poles and like the one at the water and the complex of stiff drop-fences presented maximum problems for the riders, and called for matching courage and ability by the horses, with the tight timing and extra length putting a premium on fitness. It was a brilliantly conceived course that, given a little luck, brought the best riders and horses to the fore, and proved beyond the capabilities of the others.

At the start of the cross-country the USA, Switzerland, West Germany and Britain were well in the hunt. The American Jimmy Wofford, riding as an individual, was the first to court disaster when his horse Kilkenny threw up its head after a huge leap, and hit its rider so hard in the face that he was dazed and fell off. Mary Gordon-Watson and the great Cornishman, the pathfinders for the British team, lived up to their reputation, going clear except for a stop at the 'bogy' Bank, when conflicting advice about which to jump of two equally hazardous alternatives cost them a refusal, and with it the individual bronze medal. Riding cautiously, as ordered, over the first part of the course, Cornishman went so strongly over the second half that they went into the lead for a time, until overtaken by the eventual winners of the individual medal, the Swedish Jan Jonsson with Sarajevo, who went both fast and clear. In common with many others, Cornish Gold's only stop was also at the Bank, and this was the scene of one of several disasters that overtook Mark Phillips that day.

Good horse that Great Ovation undoubtedly was, Mark is correct in not assessing him among the great ones. However well it was accomplished, this was a horse that did only what he had to do, and he lacked the willing, inspired love of the game conspicuous in horses like Cornishman and Laurieston. Ovation's apparent lack of *joie de vivre* during the previous day's dressage turned to a non-co-operative distaste for the entire cross-country, after he stood off and fell at the Parallels at fence 4, and there were two refusals and another fall at an oxer before Mark's strength and ability got them to the finishing post. The ambitions of every top-class event rider centre on the peak of the Olympics, and it was the big moment of Mark's competing life when he was chosen for the team to go to Munich. Just to be there was an honour, and no-one expects to do more than their best, which, with a little of the luck every competitor needs, can be better yet. But the form that day was true neither to horse nor rider, and this was what added frustration to disappointment.

There were plenty of others among the top echelons to share the same feelings that day. West Germany's not unfounded optimism of winning two golds, diminished when Horst Karsten and Sioux met with a series of catastrophies that culminated in elimination and concussion for the rider. Clarke Roycroft, one of the Australian team with a maximum bonus on the steeplechase behind him, also encountered disasters that ended in retirement. The good performances of two of the American team had a setback when their captain's horse, Free and Easy, fell when he missed his footing after landing safely on the notorious Bank, but they still remained the chief danger to British chances. By mid-afternoon the USA were in the lead, and Britain's fortunes lay with Richard Meade's ability to go clear in a faster time than the American team member, Kevin Freeman.

From the word go Derek Allhusen felt that in Laurieston he had an exceptional animal. The young horse seemed to have inherited all his mother's brilliance, her spring and speed and good action, but had a good temperament and was not as highly strung. In 1970, when an accident prevented Major Allhusen from riding, the six-year-old Laurieston was lent to the well-known event rider, Lorna Sutherland. She rode him well, but he is a strong man's ride that is not the type to go in any way but his own, and he refused to co-operate with the precision riding she required.

Michael Tucker was Laurieston's next rider, and he began their partnership with the distinction of being thrown off during a dressage test. However within a month they had won the senior section at Tidworth, and the selection committee had thoughts about running them in the World Championships at Burghley.

The Allhusens considered the young horse too inexperienced for such an event at that stage, but instead he was included in the 'second eleven' for the mini-Olympics at Munich. Laurieston's brilliance in all the phases there brought him and Michael Tucker into third place out of sixty or seventy horses for the individual bronze, a placing that would have been higher but for 20 technical faults incurred in a penalty area. The British team won the event, and the Allhusens could have sold their horse several times over, for almost any price they liked to name.

At the time the British Equestrian Federation were negotiating to buy a horse for Richard Meade to ride in the Munich Olympics, and Major Allhusen took the hard decision of loaning his own horse and switching Richard on to Laurieston for a trial. The immediate results were not very satisfactory. This is a horse that is so supple he jumps like a cat and can screw out of anything, but he can be very difficult to sit on. However ten days hunting before Christmas 1971 started to establish the essential confidence between rider and horse, and laid the foundations for their future success. Even so, Richard was still getting used to the horse by the beginning of the 1972 season, and their showing in the spring trials was inauspicious. Then came the great performance at Badminton where only an error of judgement over timing in the jumping phase, put them into second place. Richard Meade and Laurieston were established as a good team, and as the outstanding partnership that brought them into the starting 'box' at Munich, with clear-cut orders to go like hell, and the unenviable task of pulling all the chestnuts out of the fire. And combining all his experience and ability to ride to the occasion with a brilliant horse's courage and speed, that was an order the fourth member of the British team obeyed to the letter.

They rapped a few of the fences, but that is inevitable when a rider has to take chances, and they went clear. And because Laurieston was supremely fit, for all that he was asked to do he was still galloping with something in hand at the finish, with a final timing that was seven seconds faster than the American.

On the last day forty-eight riders remained to try their skill in the jumping arena, over a course that included three changes of rein and twelve fences, with the vertical orange and white poles at No. 2 and a narrow stile at No. 7 causing most of the trouble. Australia, suffering fewer mishaps than Switzerland, and owing to the doughty efforts of Bill Roycroft with Warrathoola and Richard Sands with Depeche, were lying fourth, West Germany third, the USA second. Britain was in the lead, both as a team and in the individual rating.

The course was straightforward but there were only a dozen clear rounds, of which Cornishman's was one, Great Ovation's another. Cornish Gold hit one fence. Richard Meade came into the arena knowing he was sitting on two gold medals – so long as the day went well.

Apart from the possibility, remote with a pair of this calibre, of faulting at so many fences that the round became a débacle, there were other mishaps that could do them down. But Laurieston did not slip up on the flat, which would have rocketed their score with 30 penalties, and Richard kept his head and did not jump a wrong fence – which happened to a luckless Russian in Mexico and entails elimination for the rider and, far worse, elimination for his team. They went clear, the British team won the Olympic Gold, Richard Meade became and remains the only rider to date to be a triple gold medallist, and Laurieston filled the Allhusens' cup of happiness to the full by laying proud and just claim to being 'one of the few great horses'.

Riding in international events as a member of a team requires a slightly different approach to riding as an individual, although in both cases rider and horse have been selected to represent their country. Like the team member the individual is expected to complete all phases if it is possible, but there is more scope for individual decision. Richard Meade is a first-rate member of a team, a brilliant strategist and a great morale booster, and as a team member he rides strictly to orders. The rider sent off as number one to pathfind the cross-country is expected to get round safely at all costs then report back on any special hazards and such vital information as the going in different sections. This may entail foregoing some otherwise legitimate risk that may 'up' an individual's score, but the team has to come first. Alternatively, when the marks are needle-tight the last member to go may have to take a number of chances in order to get the required time boost. And although in the final count only the three best scores are used, however bad the round, a team member must still continue in case another comes to irretrievable grief.

There is also another side. A team still has to think, behave and work as one when off duty. There is no more room for the 'loner' back stage than for the brilliant individualist when competing, or for anyone who is unwilling to pull his weight, whether it is in fraternizing with the opposition, or lending a hand 'studding' a team mate's horse.

In September 1975 Princess Anne was picked as a member of the first all ladies three-day event team, to contest the European Championships at Luhmuhlen in West Germany. Her competitive performance there, second only to Lucinda Prior-Palmer who took the individual championship Anne won in 1971, and as part of the team only just beaten by the Russians, resulted in a place for her and Goodwill on the short-list for Montreal. And as a good team 'trooper' she more than earned her place, riding to order, mucking in with everything that went on from chores to entertainments, and with it all thoroughly enjoying herself.

Luhmuhlen Riding Club, a type of establishment where the members keep their own horses, has been running a national three-day event for fifteen years. The Championships however were organized by Dr Specht who was responsible for Munich, and once more were a model of German efficiency with no expense spared. As would be expected the cross-country course, big enough to 'frighten the wits out of the riders' but built by horsemen determined to do everything possible to avoid hurting the horses, was expertly designed and built. There must be few other nations who would go to the trouble of constructing the water jump from scratch, making an artificial lake, the bottom sleeper lined, complete with a central island and authentic, hand planted bullrushes. The remainder of the course in places had an almost British air about it, even to the inclusion of a pheasant feeder, but that lake was something that could only be conceived and carried out with Teutonic thoroughness.

The ability to judge pace in relation to local conditions and the optimum time is an important factor in successful event riding. Too slow a speed collects penalties, going too fast takes even more out of a horse that has yet to come up next day still fit to work. Where the terrain is flat, as at Luhmuhlen, the temptation is to push up the speed, and the expert judgement of pace shown by all memers of the British team contributed to their good performance. As in Mexico, altitude is something that has to be most

Bold and careful jumping – a hallmark of a good eventer – Tidworth, 1976.

Lucinda Prior-Palmer and Be Fair at the Brigstock Horse Trials, 1976.

A novice pair parting company at the Rushall Horse Trials, 1973.

Mutual confidence between rider and horse is the essence of eventing – Princess Anne and Doublet competing in the showjumping phase at Crookham, 1972.

When the going is not so good! Badminton, washed out, 1975.

Water therapy for the Queen's horse Goodwill.

Wherever 'English' riding is practised in America combined training is now the up and coming sport – spectators at the Ledyard Trials, 1975.

British riders at the Kiev European Championships, 1973. *Left to Right:* Roslyn Jones, Marjorie Comerford, Janet Hodgson, Richard Meade, Debbie West, Princess Anne, Lucinda Prior-Palmer.

OPPOSITE Sue Hatherly weighing in at the Ledyard Horse Trials, 1975.

Expert tuition for the younger generation of eventers? Alison Oliver with her son Philip.

carefully taken into account, and was a problem being tackled by all teams bound for Bromont in July 1976.

The weather is another important matter, if one that cannot be controlled, and it can change the entire aspect of an event and upset all preconceived ideas on how to ride a cross-country course, as competitors in the Dutch Trials at Boekelo in 1974 and 1975 discovered.

For centuries the Dutch were known more for dealing in horses than for riding them, but the scene is a very different one today. There are hundreds of Pony Clubs, the equine element mostly provided by the popular British pony breeds, the number of riding clubs increases yearly, and competitions in dressage, show jumping and driving are held throughout the country. The Three-Day trials at Boekelo are a widely popular date, and eleven nationalities were competing in 1974 when Britain sent thirteen representatives.

There had been nothing untoward about either weather or going in 1973, when Britain won the team title from the French, and there were five Britons amongst the first six places. The old rivals, Richard Meade and Mark Phillips, headed the list, the four-fifths of a penalty in Richard's favour preventing Mark from achieving his fourth three-day event win of the year. Goodwill fell on the steeplechase, and Anne is reported to have commented that the Dutch earth was less hard than the Russian. At least it was not waterlogged as in 1974.

That year it was fine on cross-country day but up to then had been teeming with rain, necessitating shortening the mud-bath of the steeplechase track and cutting out a 700 metre loop of marshy ground on the cross-country, plus a couple of fences. An island fence also had to go, and the large pond effect that started as the first part of a double over a ditch. Even so the mud and slosh caused innumerable falls, and a dive into the lake for Sue Hatherly when Maribou used the take-off platform as a springboard, and lost his footing as he resurfaced.

Fortunately it takes more than bad weather and a few falls to deter event riders. A good time was had by all, and Britain's troop of young riders and horses gained valuable experience and came third to France and Germany.

In 1975 it was fog, swirling, clammy fog that greeted the starters at Boekelo, with at least one competitor losing his way on the steeplechase course, and the start of the cross-country delayed by two and a half hours. The going was good however, although only Lucinda Prior-Palmer and Wideawake came seventeen seconds under time, and their bold jumping of fences looming up in the murk exacting no more penalties, then or in the jumping phase, to add to a winning dressage mark of 46. Richard Meade with Jacob Jones was third, and Sue Hatherly, despite another impromptu bath in the lake, managed to finish fourteenth out of twenty-one. The British team won, including amongst their trophies two metres of currant loaf.

In 1836 there was heavy betting against the arrival on time of the eventual winner of the St Leger, being transported in the first ever horse-drawn, horse box from Goodwood. A far cry from the modern forms of travel that make competing abroad feasible, especially for the international teams and riders for whom the organizing committee are responsible. The British team horses for Luhmuhlen sailed from Harwich in the evening, arriving at Bremerhaven the next morning to continue their journey by road.

There are several firms that specialize in horse transport, loading the animals in England into big, comfortable horse boxes and delivering them to their destination on the Continent without change of vehicle. One of the most relaxed and cheapest methods of travelling horses across Europe is by rail – provided that all goes well. An occasion when things did not go according to plan was in 1974, when the British team animals for the Junior European Championships being held in Italy, once across the Channel were loaded into French cattle trucks, and hitched to a *rapide*, a train that keeps going but without the extra speed that bounces the horses too much for their good. All went well until the Italian border where the trucks were incorporated as part of a goods train and horses and their devoted grooms were then 'lost' for twelve hours. Fortunately they turned up in time, and in quite good order considering they had spent half a day with little water and under a broiling sun, being shunted in and out of marshalling yards.

Nowadays the sophisticated arrangements for flying horses here and there around the world mean that new fields are there for the conquering, even for riders domiciled thousands of miles away. Curiously, few horses take much exception to a form of transport that equates them with Pegasus, and equine passengers are 'regulars' on the various airlines, most of them racehorses, or brood mares visiting foreign based stallions. Now that they travel by jet the horses, like general cargo, are 'palletized'. This means they are loaded on the ground into their flying stalls, usually two or three joined together that are then stowed on wooden pallets and pushed on to a fork lift by means of roller bearings. Raised to the height of the plane's loading door the pallets can then be trundled into position in the tail over the roller bearings that cover the floor. The horses are accompanied by their grooms and can be under constant supervision, and the majority spend the flight contentedly munching hay, and free of the continual bracing necessary when brakes are going on and off during transport by road.

Even in the days when air travel, for humans as well as horses, was considerably less comfortable, once aboard the plane the majority of the horses stayed calm – but there are exceptions, and thousands of feet above the earth is not the best place to meet up with one.

After a never-forgotten journey in a horse box, following being staked in the chest when hunting, Richard Meade's Barberry was always inclined to suffer from claustrophobia when travelling. During a journey across the Channel he became panicky and smashed the partition, but fortunately arrived unscathed despite thrusting his forelegs through into the cab beside the driver. Yet he remained calm on the flight to Tokyo for the Olympics in 1964, and when the first ever equestrian team to Russia set out to contest the European Championships held there in the following year, it was Derek Allhusen's Lochinvar who played up. In fact he behaved so badly shortly after take-of that a special box, made for transporting the show jumper Firecrest to Tokyo, was flown out for the return journey.

In those days, without pallets and fork lifts, the horses had to walk up a ramp into the plane, and then into the narrow stalls that are the safest for flying. Once airborn, Lochinvar, who had never flown before, kept trying to lie down in the restricted space, and since he would undoubtedly have become stuck and injured had he succeeded, those in charge had a hectic flight hanging on to the slings they had managed to insert under the horse's stomach, and literally holding him up on his feet. Their troubles were not over when the transport plane touched down at Moscow airport, only fifteen minutes after the arrival of the plane bringing the riders and rest of the entourage. The horses had to come off the plane by the same ramp they had gone in by, the ramp had to be positioned by a crane, and it took the Russians three and a half hours to produce one. By then it was 2.00 am, and one horse having surveyed Russia from the top of the ramp promptly decided he thought little of the view and would rather take a return flight home. By 4.00 am all the horses were actually on the ground, but there was still a thirty-mile drive to the allotted stabling at the main racing stadium in Moscow.

Obviously Russian horses are not pampered like the degenerate creatures of the West, and the transport provided for this journey consisted of a convoy of Army lorries, each divided into two by a tubular rail, with no tops, sides two feet high and bare metal floors. To get aboard each horse had to be persuaded to walk up the same ramp, taken from the plane, and once in they stood facing forwards. A little hay was scrounged from the plane for them to stand on, and the convoy set off, the riders sitting on small benches, their backs to the cab and each with a horse's head in his lap. Everyone had visions of their animals jumping out en route as the vehicles rattled and swayed round the corners, low-hanging branches hitting the occupants in the face, and their speed determined by the young soldier drivers all impatient for their long delayed breakfast. But the horses, even Lochnivar and Barberry, never batted an eyelid – maybe they were as tired as their attendants – and once at the stadium the whole scene changed.

For a start, the stabling was first-rate, and included such forethought as automatic drinking bowls and wood shavings for bedding, and the entire competition proved to be both well organized and enjoyable. Foreign steeplechase courses seldom bear much resemblance to British ones, but it was the riders more than the horses who were surprised to meet in this phase an assortment of odd obstacles, including walls set on banks and a huge brush fence with a 5 foot 6 inch ditch in front of it. But the going was fast and good and the cross-country, like that at Kiev eight years later, relatively straightforward and well-constructed. There were a few Russian touches to liven things up, such as rounding a corner to come suddenly on a wooden bank painted bright red, and leaping down into a river and then trotting along to the next fence that was an upturned boat, pegged down so that its sides just touched the water.

The Russians mostly ride stallions, tough little horses that jump like cats and are capable of most attractive dressage. When they compete abroad the horses sometimes appear to be suffering from over-training, or from fatigue from their mode of transport that can involve a long, slow train journey, or something approaching the saga with the elderly truck that was driven all the way from Moscow and broke down several times en route. At the trials in Moscow horses and riders had the usual advantage of the host nation being on home ground, but they put up an excellent performance to win, with Ireland second and Great Britain third. From the Russian point of view it was all a most worthwhile rehearsal for the 1973 championships in Kiev. That was when Yevdokimov and his brown thoroughbred Jeger, in their first international challenge, won the individual medal, and the Russian team came second to Germany in an event considerably more sophisticated than that in 1965, and one of considerably more importance to the Russian people.

Because of stringent quarantine restrictions against horse sickness, even air transport cannot give European riders the chance of competing with their own animals in South Africa, or South Africans the same opportunities in England and on the Continent, and this is a pity from all points of view. The climax of the South African eventing season is the Whitbread Cup, two-day trials that are organized on the wide-open spaces of the veldt north of Johannesburg. In addition to the national talent competitors come from some neighbouring African countries, and in 1974 Jane Bullen and Chris Collins had the happy opportunity of joining them on loaned horses.

There was little time to become acquainted with their mounts, but after creditable dressage tests on the first day, performed under the blue of African skies, the heat of the sun tempered by a breeze and the high altitude, the British riders prepared to meet the challenges of the morrow.

The $4\frac{1}{2}$-mile cross-country was a tough course, the hard going made hazardous for the uninitiated with slabs of bare rock, holes, stones, and a marshy donga formed by soil erosion. The thirty-one fences many with strange African names, included a 10 foot drop off a bank and several big parallels, but the most adventurous involved swimming across a dam. Jane Bullen had a fall and one stop, but still finished seventh in the final placings. Chris Collins, whose exploits in the field of equitation include winning Czechoslovakia's notorious Grand Pardubice steeplechase, achieved one of the three clears out of seventeen starters to finish the day in third place.

In Australia the long distances involved have a bearing on national combined training competitions, and internationally they are also once more affected by the stringent quarantine regulations. Nevertheless, due partly to an enthusiastic and thriving Pony Club, and boosted sky high by the winning of a gold medal in the 1960 Olympics, eventing in the various states is on the 'up', and Australian riders continue to make their mark on the international scene.

Originally dressage was more of a bugbear 'down under' than it was in England. From the time the first settlers started importing horses, the animals were used for travelling immense distances, either as pure transport or as stock horses. Endurance, and the ability of both rider and horse to go fast across rough country when necessary, were the qualities that counted, and largely remained so after mechanization relegated the majority of horses to the realms of pleasure riding. The disciplines of dressage are far removed from the natural Australian seat or concept of horsemanship, and there seemed little necessity for a form of training, practised in Europe for centuries, but neither admired nor understood in a land so many thousands of miles away.

The first-ever one-day horse trial took place in 1951 and caused little stir.

But when Australia became host nation for the Olympics in 1956, although the equestrian events were organized in Stockholm there was an obligation for Australian riders to take part, and it was imperative that they and their horses acquire a knowledge of dressage. Instructors were discovered amongst the newly arrived European immigrants, and a nucleus of Australian riders, quite legitimately confident of their own and their horses' capacity to jump across country, set out to learn the rudiments of an art still considered by many to be not quite 'manly'.

At the invitation of the British Horse Society the six riders who formed the first Australian Olympic team spent the previous year with their trainer in England. Laurie Morgan also brought his horse over at his own expense, and scored the first Australian overseas success with a win in the Windsor Three-Day Event, held as the final trials before Stockholm.

It said much for the courage and fitness of the Australians and their horses, and for the thorough training they had received, that the team came fourth in their first Olympics, but better showing in the dressage phase would have won Australia the bronze medal. Those who watched the event saw the lesson rammed home by the disparity between the team's tests and that performed by the Swedish rider, Major St Cyr, who won the individual gold and captained his team to victory. Back home the point was taken by those who, up to then had been convinced dressage to European standards was not essential for success in combined training, and as a direct result of the Olympics three-day events were introduced into Australia. The first full-sized affair was organized at the Sydney Easter Royal Show, where it became a permanency, and it was there that Bill Roycroft, a name that belongs to the annals of the sport, first came to prominence.

Despite the changed outlook the dressage results were disappointing in the 1960 Rome Olympics, but the Australians' speed and skill on the steeplechase put them into the lead. Laurie Morgan's brilliant and unbeatable time over the cross-country then kept them in the same position, despite a rider having to continue with a broken collar-bone, and the breakdown of one horse. Overall victory was made possible only by Bill Roycroft escaping from hospital to complete the team for the final phase. Their eventual 260 point victory over Switzerland who came second, with France third and Britain fourth, with both the gold and silver in the individual table as well, impressed the world with the Australian riders' courage and indomitable determination.

Four years later in Tokyo a poor showing in the dressage phase yet again followed by disasters for two riders across country spoilt the record. But at

Mexico City, despite worse dressage scores and the calamitous deluge during the cross-country, the Australian team, which included Bill Roycroft and his son Clarke, came third to take the bronze medal. Four years later at Munich the team was fourth, with the only other plus score.

Badminton has been a happy hunting ground for Australian riders on several occasions, particularly in 1960 when Bill Roycroft and Our Solo put on a very attractive demonstration of dressage and then took the final honours, and again in 1961 when Laurie Morgan and Salad Days repeated the effort. Bill, an evergreen competitor well into his fifties, was at Badminton again in 1969, but sadly got no further than the Lake where he removed his horse's bridle with him, and then had to watch the unfeeling animal going for a swim in the nude. There were no Australians actually competing in the 1974 World Championship at Burghley, but with the American, Beth Perkins, riding Furtive, Clarke Roycroft's former Olympic horse, and with Hugh Thomas and Playamar both trained by Australia's former Olympic rider Brian Crago, going so well there and at Badminton in 1976, it could be said Australia had at least a finger in the pie.

In Australia today combined training is an increasingly popular sport. At Pony Club level a State Championship One-Day Event is held in some states, and many have adult Horse Trial Clubs providing facilities for training, usually comprising dressage instruction followed by cross-country work. Interest in dressage is on the increase, even as a sport on its own, and in 1974 the Lipizzaner stallion, Siglavi Flora II, and some mares, were imported from the Spanish School in Vienna as a nucleus for breeding the horses that, above all others, are exponents of the classical art of *haute école*.

All the Australian states promote one-day eventing at open, novice, and sometimes maiden levels, and three-day events are held annually in New South Wales, Victoria and South Australia, and on occasions in the remaining states. In general the Australians ride thoroughbreds for the sport that are mostly not very big animals, but neat and agile and with the superb natural balance that makes them such good show jumpers. Apart from the horse trial clubs, they are normally schooled on their owners' properties and, like most others, gain their experience by actual competing.

The Americans have been competing at international level for a long time. They were third in the Olympics at Stockholm in 1912, they won in 1932 when the Games were staged in Los Angeles, and took the individual silver, and the team gold in 1948 at Aldershot, the year when a few British riders started to sit up and take notice of the sport. In Helsinki 1932 the Americans were back in third position again, but out of the placings in 1956 and 1960. Tokyo, Mexico and Munich brought them the silver medal on each occasion, but Montreal 1976 has given them opportunity to forsake the position of bridesmaid for that of the bride once more.

In 1974 the USA sent a team to Burghley to compete in the World Championship. It consisted of Denny Emerson with Victor Dakin, Don Sachy riding the Olympic veteran Plain Sailing, and the horse's Munich pilot, the up-and-coming young Bruce Davidson this time with Irish Cap. Their captain was the experienced Mike Plumb with Good Mixture, another reliable member of the Munich squad.

Bruce Davidson was born in New England and started riding a pony when he was six. Three years later he took over a large horse that happened to be available, but really started getting to grips with some of the basics of riding when, having reverted to a 13 h.h. pony, he joined a Pony Club in New York State. At about the same age he began fox-hunting regularly during the appropriate holidays, a sport he still indulges whenever possible, and while at school gained a lot of experience in various forms of competing, including eventing. After competing in one of the screening trials held in the USA following each Olympic Games to find young riders of promise, Bruce was picked to stay on for training at Gladstone, the centre in New Jersey that the eventing team formerly shared with the show jumpers. He remained there for nearly three years, riding team horses and eventually Plain Sailing, that he then rode in the Canadian Championships of 1971, and breaking in his own Irish bred and suitably named Irish Cap.

Married to Carol Hannum, a leading lady rider of similar eventing interests, Bruce now farms in Pennsylvania. He also breeds high class horses more or less as a hobby, as with Irish Cap, making them from scratch, and then schooling them on for whatever role they seem best suited, be it dressage horse, eventer, or point-to-pointer.

Early in 1974 Bruce and his wife, her horse Paddy and Irish Cap, came to England and spent the first few months in a cottage near Wylye, imbibing the British attitude towards eventing, and with Badminton as the immediate goal. A try-out in Devon, at the Ermington Trials, resulted in a win, and at Badminton Bruce and Irish Cap came third below Mark Phillips and Columbus, and Janet Hodgson with Larkspur. It was a pointer to where the chief British opposition in the World Championships could be expected.

After a couple of months back home Bruce returned for a three month training stint with the USA world cup team, under the brilliant instruction of Jack le Goff, Olympic rider on two occasions and twice champion of France, who has also stimulated Bruce Davidson's interest in pure dressage, and in his other love, show jumping.

On the subject of the relative importance of the various phases in three-day eventing, Bruce shares the outlook of the leading British riders, that although the cross-country remains the dominant factor, to win at today's standards of World Championships and the Olympics, it is not sufficient for a horse just to be exceptional and fast across country, it has got to be equally good in the dressage and jumping arenas. When it comes to comparing the overall standard in the two countries, except at the top strata where there is now little to choose between them, the level of work on the ground is lower in England than in the States, but at preliminary and intermediate stages the British riders and horses have the edge on the Americans in their innate ability to go across country.

Basically the American approach to dressage training is slightly different to that of the British, and to that of the Australians, but while this does achieve a superficially different result, at top international level it still meets the same requirements. Many Australian horses are now capable of top class dressage in events, but they are trained and ridden with the individual approach that is as much a British characteristic as an Australian one. American eventers, riders and horses, are trained to a pattern, and a very good pattern at that, in the same way that all riders and horses in those American states where 'English riding' is practised, come out of the same mould.

The American world team had the advantage of the national aptitude for being meticulously thorough, and of being very well-trained as a team, and they arrived at Burghley as well-prepared for a world competition as any four riders and horses could be. Bruce Davidson had ridden his wife's Paddy to victory at the Brahmam Park three-day event in Yorkshire two weeks previously, and he was the most obvious danger to Mark Phillips and the reformed Columbus.

Ten nations were concerned, and by the end of the two days of dressage the team placings were headed by West Germany followed by Britain, and then France fractionally ahead of the USA.

The speed and endurance test covered a little under 18 miles, the cross-country accounting for nearly 5 of them. The steeplechase caused trouble for some, but although a proportion of the thirty-two big, solid cross-country fences may have appeared strange to Russian, Polish and other foreign eyes, and there were numerous falls and eliminations, one or two bogy jumps and several total immersions and an amount of grief at the Trout Hatchery, the Americans acquitted themselves with honour. Don Sachey and Plain Sailing had a fall at the Sleeper Wall-and-Bank, Denny Emmerson collected more time faults than the other two, on a course where getting the quickest way over a fence was more time-saving than sheer speed on the flat. Otherwise the team found few real problems and the course rode much as they thought it would.

The Double Coffin gave them no worries, the Lapped Rails, jumped from sunlight into woodland, often an unpopular aspect to a horse, did not deter the Americans. An Irish horse tried to bank the Log-Pile with dire results, another fell here and one refused, but the riders from the USA, keeping hold of the front end, riding forward and retaining their horses in balance, had that obstacle behind them without trouble. Those Park Gates at the end of a downward slope and with a sharp turn into them, they were solid and straight up and down at 3 feet 11 inches, and a lot of horses clouted them good and hard. But it was a question of meeting them right, and then swinging correctly uphill for a good approach to the big combination of the Dairy Rails at the top, where there was a big drop down over the off-bank side and a crowd of spectators to mask the exit for the horse. There was a lot of thought about how to jump the Bull Pens at Nos 16 and 17. It was a rough riding obstacle taken as three separate elements, but worse attempting to go across the corner. None of the four competitors who tried that route succeeded, and that was where Britain's Bridget Parker and Cornish Gold had their only stop. Those Steps going up and down No. 19 could be a real horse problem, as three discovered to their cost, and the 13 feet of open water demanded no loss of impulsion if the horses were not to jump into it. In the home straight the Zig-Zag Rails at No. 28 needed to be treated with respect, and the Double Rails at No. 30 were every bit as high and wide as they appeared and a formidable obstacle for a tiring horse. Then it was cope with the Trakener and take no chances with the last one, that welcome Raleigh Chopper, one last gallop, and home and dry.

That was how it went for Bruce Davidson, clear and 8 time faults slower than Mark Phillips and Columbus who were only twenty seconds outside the optimum time. That was how it went for the team captain, Mike Plumb, with the experience of four Olympics behind him. Next day by the end of the jumping phase the Americans were confirmed in their gold for the team.

It had promised to be a ding-dong match between Bruce and Mark for the individual gold medal, with Mark starting off in the lead, but Columbus had put paid to British chances long before the show jumping began. They had worked all night on the ligament which slipped off his hock at the penultimate fence on the cross-country, and by morning success seemed a possibility, but the horse, a strange individual, one that always hated to be looked at, kicked out at someone passing behind him and undid all the good work, and more. So the Americans returned home in triumph bearing the World Championship team gold medal, with Bruce Davidson the individual World Champion, and Mike Plumb only ·26 penalties behind him with the silver. It had been a good trip.

Combined training is now an up-and-coming sport in America, but because of the vast areas involved and the differences in conditions and climate and interests of the various states, the sport remains a more or less unknown quantity in many parts. Obviously eventing is not a sport for those who ride 'western', and except for California where every style of riding flourishes, and a few other states such as Texas and New Mexico where the 'English seat' is not unknown, the majority of American horse trials are centred in the middle Atlantic states.

The United States Pony Club sponsors a large number of one-day trials for its members, and there are numerous adult one-day competitions at which the pre-training and training divisions roughly approximate to the same standards as those put on by the British Riding Clubs. In all, around 130 one-day trials and a few two-day are organized annually throughout the seven designated eventing areas, a proportion classified as official by the Events Committee of the American Horse Show Association.

In addition there are three official three-day trials, the Radnor Hunt Three-Day Event held in Pennsylvania in June, the Flying Horse Horse-Trials at South Hamilton in the fall, and, best known of all, the three-day event at Ledyard Farm, Massachusetts, close by the US Equestrian team's training centre, that takes place every two years.

For the American eventing fraternity one of the big results of the Ledyard Trials in 1973, was the boost given to the sport by the competition actually being reported, albeit shortly, in the *New York Times*. In 1975 when the event for the second time was organized at international level, ticket sales, enthusiasm and excitement were way above anything experienced before, and during the three days concerned an estimated 140,000 spectators, the majority first-timers, came to have their fill of the thrills and skills attached to eventing at various standards. The opportunity also to watch the Myopia Three-Day Driving Event and a high goal polo match gave the crowds their money's worth, but it was the advanced level Horse Trials Championship that was the big draw.

Teams flew in from Canada, West Germany and Holland to compete in the most outstanding horse trials, outside the 1932 Olympics, yet offered in the USA, and six horses and riders had been invited from Britain. The contingent consisted of Princess Anne and Mark, Lucinda Prior-Palmer, Sue Hatherly, Janet Hodgson, and Michael Tucker. Sue's Harley, along with her to defend their title won in 1973, was the only really seasoned horse. Anne's Arthur of Troy had only done a few trials and one intermediate three-day event and for Mark's Laureate II, Lucinda's Wideawake, Janet's Gretna Green and Mike's Ben Wyvis, this was also a first international competition. Added to their inexperience were the problems, common to all the foreign horses, of jet-lag and unaccustomed summer heat.

A week before the event the six British, two Dutch and two German horses were flown in to Kennedy Airport, with their allotted quota of grooms, one for two horses, and in the expert care of Peter Scott-Dunn, veterinary surgeon to the British team and an indispensible part of it. After a stop-off at the quarantine station in New Jersey for blood tests, the contingent arrived late on the night of Saturday, 21 June, safely but very tired, at the Ledyard Farm Stables, where they welcomed a supplementary groom force of four American Pony Clubbers, a former three-day event groom, and a German speaking Canadian, all provided as volunteers, and predictably efficient. The foreign riders arrived the next day, including Mark and Anne and their trainer Alison Oliver who were soon assuring themselves of their horses' well-being in what was nicknamed the 'International Barn'. The tempo for the days in hand began to quicken.

The excellent facilities provided for exercising, schooling and practising dressage were soon sorted out, and those for swimming and cooling off by the pool, and sampling the good meals available at the nearby 'Party Barn', equally appreciated. Horses were provided, thirty-six in all loaned by members of the Myopia Hunt, for the advanced competitors to ride, while learning and inwardly digesting the routes for the roads and tracks. One of these was commandeered by Anne's detective, a conscientious and sporting, if basically unhorseminded man, who returned from the two-hour ride smiling and unbowed, but minus a proportion of skin.

Apart from the officers accompanying Anne and Mark out from England, there had to be tight local security, but this was something that, like the astonishing efficiency of the entire Ledyard 1975 set-up, in no way diminished the pervading relaxed and friendly atmosphere. A happy feeling that dominated the scene and was much appreciated by all the foreign visitors, whether wandering in and out of the barn seeing to their horses, joining with gusto in the after work hospitality, or busy on the day's stint of training.

There were two television crews, one British, one American, busily filming a detailed account of everything that went on up to as well as including the actual competition. Like the WMLO radio, which provided a live transmission throughout the Essex County area for the entire cross-country section of the event, they were out to put over the sport in a big way to a previously uncomprehending American public. They too were provided with horses for seeking out good locations to best picture the roads and tracks section of the endurance phase, but Colonel Bill Lithgow, the British *Chef d'Equipe*, utilized that mechanized equine-of-all-work, a Mini-Moke, to make a recce of ground fit for galloping his team's horses. In American eyes the British pamper their animals' feet when it comes to considering what is suitable going for fast training, but the old Willowdale Race Course proved a satisfactory choice. The British contingent were boxed there on the Tuesday for an early morning warm-up followed by a pipe-opening breeze, and the day concluded late with a convivial and mouth-watering New England clambake.

The other foreigners did their galloping at Willowdale on the Wednesday. On the next day the British team returned for a half hour trot and canter before the final 3 furlongs at speed, setting off at 5.00 am in order to have the horses washed and cooled off ready for a veterinary inspection back at the horse barn by 8.45 am.

Friday was dressage day.

By then the crowds of other competitors, officials, grooms and authorized volunteers were well-used to seeing Anne and Mark around in the casual shirts and jeans they, like everyone else, wear for everyday work with the horses. But there was a lot of admiration for Anne's turn-out when she appeared in the dressage full rig of top hat and tail coat ('shad belly' to an American), and for Mark in his uniform of the First The Queen's Dragoon Guards.

End of dressage day. Mark and Laureate were in the lead after a first-class test, a German close behind, then the American rider Beth Perkins with Furtive, another German lying fourth. Gretna Green, Ben Wyvis and Wideawake were all in contention. Bruce Davidson, deprived by illness of Irish Cap, succeeded in being one of the top-liners with Golden Griffin, an English thoroughbred eight-day acquaintance, bought for the American event team, that originated with Bertie Hill. Anne, subjected to a noisier-than-usual whirring and clicking from a barrage of movie and still cameras, was pleased that Arthur, always inclined to be too conscious of crowds and to get up-tight when competing, settled sufficiently to keep their marks within the first ten. Sue Hatherly and Harvey were 0·25 penalties behind them. It could be anybody's championship.

Roads and tracks are designed, like the other endurance phases, as a test of stamina, obedience and capability, and at Ledyard they had it right. The roads section included some of the hazards normal to modern road riding, the well flagged tracks included hills and valleys, a ditch, water and variations in tough going.

One competitor had retired during the dressage test, but none of the remaining thirty-one starters got lost, and Anne, setting off twenty minutes after her husband, was glad to realize by the feel of her horse that Arthur was 'on the ball', enjoying himself, ready for what was to come. Her timing was good with two and a half minutes in hand, then it was into the starting 'box' for the steeplechase, with the fervent hope that Arthur would not indulge his old habit of occasionally standing up on his hind legs, or the later peculiarity when under stress of setting off in reverse instead of forwards. He did neither, but concentrated on the job in hand, going a good gallop and taking every fence as he should. As they came to the finish the horse tried a speedy duck out in the direction of his stable but Anne was too quick for him, bringing him round to the buckets and the helpers waiting to sponge him down before they set off again on the second lap of tracks.

Mark and Laureate had enjoyed their steeplechasing too and were on schedule with phase C, comprising the 6 miles back to Ledyard Farm, before embarking on the cross-country. But poor Janet Hodgson had brought Gretna Green those thousands of miles to compete, only to have to withdraw after phase C when the mare suffered a muscle spasm.

When they walked the course, like the majority of the competitors Mark and Anne had been very impressed. She was struck in particular with the variety of the fences, beautifully constructed with round, flat or natural bark rails, fences painted white, proper stone walls, and proper green hedges. They were all big, if not quite as big as Badminton, well thought out and pleasing to look at. The four problem fences were well spaced, and required a lot of thought about how best to ride them, especially the Puzzle at No. 6, and that difficult combination, the Stolen 'S' at No. 26. There was colour and diversity of shape about the fences, and the all-over American flavour added to the attractions of the course.

Back from phase C for the vet check and ten minute break, that most important opportunity to refresh the horse before the cross-country, Anne handed Arthur over to be checked and washed off and scraped, and sat for a moment's rest in the cool. That was when Mark appeared to give the unbelievable news that he was eliminated.

With this rider and horse it really did seem incredible, but there it was and this is how the sport can go even for the top-notchers. Laureate had dealt with the Motif Number One, the Zig-Zag and Munich Pen, he had coped with the Helsinki, the Hard Hack Rails, the Birch Rail Bounce, he had gone all the way to, and over, the Stock Tanks, but increasingly Mark had felt there was something about the horse and its mouth that was not quite right. And after a third refusal at the next fence, the Coffin at No. 14 that spelled elimination, he discovered what it was. For the first time ever Laureate had managed to get his tongue over the bit, an operation that is uncomfortable for the horse and upsets the rider's general control and ability to communicate and place the animal's head. At Ledyard 1973 Mark's horse, Maid Marian, had broken down on the steeplechase. Maybe in 1977 the luck will be with him.

For Anne the news was a bit shattering but it also put her more than ever on her metal. She could not possibly let the side down now, and she and Arthur had better get cracking. As usual the horse was finding the crowds a little strange and was liable to stare about him instead of concentrating, but he galloped on strongly, and there were few worries behind them as they came to the Puzzle, the first real problem, at an angle. Arthur coped easily with the in and out, and so it went all the way round, the horse really paying attention to what was being asked of him. He dealt neatly with the Irish Bank, an obstacle that was new to him, bounced in and out of the Birch Rails, and really flew over the Stacked Poles. Anne put every bit of determination she had into riding at the scene of Mark's disaster. Arthur jumped in well, and leaped out so big he nearly left his rider behind, but it was a comfort to have that Coffin out of the way. Where there were crowds and clapping the horse still tended to be amazed, and because of his inexperience there was no question of trying for optimum time. Anne took him steadily where it was necessary, checking him a little and giving him a few half-halts with a lot of leg to make him attend, particularly at the drop fences which were not favourite obstacles, and as usual he splashed down into the water at the Swimming Pool without a care in the world.

In the end, with only 24 time faults, it added up to a most satisfactory round and eighth place. Unfortunately a couple of fences down in the final phase the next day, dropped them down to tenth, but this was at least one of the occasions where Princess Anne was well pleased with the performance, and future potential, of her thoroughbred horse Arthur of Troy.

The defending US Open Champions, Sue Hatherly and Harley, with the second fastest time over the cross-country, had moved into third place by the end of that day, and with a clear in the show jumping concluded the competition in second place. Mick Tucker and Ben Wyvis came fifth, Lucinda and Wideawake eighth. Beth Perkins, second to Mark Phillips in the dressage, came into the stadium jumping with victory in her grasp – if she could go clear. The experienced old trooper, Furtive, had been in his element across country, but although show jumps had never been particularly to his liking, that day he was on his mettle. Clear and with only three to go it was the overnight rain that defeated them. Furtive slipped as he took off out of the pen, jumped big and twisted, dropping his shoulder and pitching his rider over his head – and Bruce Davidson with Golden Griffin became the new champions of Ledyard 1975.

The Canadians had been at Ledyard, competing with distinction in those divisions best suited to their Olympic training programme. Another, somewhat different part of the Olympic programme, the so-called mini-Olympics had been held in Montreal earlier in 1975.

This was a trial run for much of the Games. Many athletes had been there to give the organizers a chance to rehearse the arrangements for that side of it. For the three-day event operators there was the essential opportunity to see how the terrain worked out, whether the steeplechase was positioned correctly, how the ideas for crowd control could be bettered, whether the stabling side was going to function smoothly. The same idea was operated successfully before the Munich Olympics, and on such occasions different countries are invited to send competitors.

Canada most hospitably invited two British riders, all expenses paid, and Virginia Holgate, whose Jason happened to be fully fit at the time, was one of the lucky ones. Sadly the other horse went lame, but Virginia set off in state with Jason, with her mother for company and Richard Meade acting as *Chef d' Equipe*.

The site for the Games is a big and beautiful valley, used as a ski resort in winter. For the mini-competition the dressage and show jumping arenas, and the complex of roads ad tracks, were the same as those to be used in 1976, but the cross-country was an entirely different proposition. In size the fences were mid-way between Tidworth and Burghley, and the course, most imaginatively conceived, was on part of the overall trail that has been gouged out of the side of the mountain. It led along the valley, then up and along the mountain side before descending to the flat again, and many of the solid, beautifully constructed obstacles had to be jumped up or down hill, calling for a clever, bold horse and a cool-headed rider. One teaser consisted of jumping into the artificially constructed lake, leaping up on to a bridge that spans it, and then back into the water.

Before she started the competition Virginia had good cause to appreciate the vital role played by a good *Chef d' Equipe* on these occasions. Misled by an an alteration in the timings, she was enjoying her lunch when another announcement made her realize she should have been riding Jason in before his test. This is a horse that requires a lot of working in before going into the arena, and Virginia set off on the ten-minute hack to the stadium in a true flat-spin, convinced that she had lost any chances of doing a good test. By the time they reached the stadium Jason was blown up, in such a state of excitement he did not know which way he was facing, but there was Richard, cool, calm and collected, telling Virginia not to worry, that everything would be all right, and giving the advice that saved the day. As she began on a hurried work-in it was quickly obvious that Jason was not going to co-operate, either then or later. Virginia was in despair, but she was told by her experienced *Chef d' Equipe* to abandon all her normal schooling and just ride the horse in wide serpentines at rising trot – and it worked. As they entered the arena the horse was still visibly excited, but it was an animation that could be contained and gave him a lot of 'presence'. Jason performed the best dressage test of his career, and the good marks they obtained carried them through the days. Fast and clear on the steeplechase, fast and clear across country and clear again in the show jumping, and the Canadian mini-Olympics became a British victory.

Only a year later all the nations gathering together for the Olympic Games would be there in that valley in Montreal, and with them would be the world's finest riders competing in the world's toughest, most worthwhile three-day horse trials.

Conclusion

To the young rider hell-bent on competing in a first-time Pony Club Horse
Trial, to the horse owner who likes to extend active and exciting riding
beyond the local show or the hunting field, by eventing on the occasional
Saturday afternoon, the three-day event in the Olympic Games seldom
appears of more than academic interest. No event enthusiast would miss
watching those three days on television or fail to become involved with all
the emotional excitement and suspense, the admiration and patriotic
urgings, with all the saga of four- and two-legged courage that makes it a
'must' for horsemen the world over, but few really appreciate the
relationship between their own level of the sport and this Olympian battle of
the giants.

To remain in a healthy state of public interest and expansion, combined
training like most sports needs to be in the forefront, and requires boosting to
get there. Good publicity is vital to the future of eventing, and because all
facets of the sport are interdependent this is not just at the top, but for the
well-being of all the one-day horse trials now held throughout the country
during the season. And these are made possible by the generosity of sponsors
and the good efforts of hard working organizers, all of whom like the other
indispensible backers, need to be convinced that their efforts are furthering
something that is really worthwhile.

Despite questions overhanging the exact interpretation of amateur status,
the Olympic Games are the zenith of amateur competition, and remain a
shop window on the world of sport that is world-wide and has retained its
unique status for centuries. To have teams and individuals competing at
international and Olympic level is of great importance to those participating
at less exalted standards back home. And if success in a materialistic world has
almost, but not quite, superceded the famous principle of it being more
important to take part than to win, maybe gold medals do tend to speak even
louder than unadorned honour and glory. For Great Britain to win the
Olympic three-day event, is to stimulate everything and everyone connected with the sport right down to the lowest rungs of the ladder, and to

plant combined training right bang in the centre of the public eye.

This being so it seems ridiculous and short-sighted to debar from the Olympics by rigid and out-of-date rulings concerning amateur status, many of those top-class horsemen, and by inference many top-class horses, who should by right and sheer ability be among the first to be selected to represent their country. This is not to suggest inclusion of riders who, like some professional show jumpers earn their entire living from competing in their chosen sport. For many reasons, the prolonged training, the impossibility of providing sufficient events, or of an event horse being physically capable of competing in a sufficient number if there were, eventing is never likely at any level to become the province of this type of professionalism. But top standard three-day eventing is not a very cheap sport and the costs rise as national and world monetary troubles increase. The essential training involved is also sufficiently time-consuming to make it difficult for a rider of this calibre and particularly for a man, to earn his living by 'outside' means. And these are the people who could have a chance both of achieving their ultimate ambition, to compete in the Olympic Games, and of solving the inevitable monetary problem if they were allowed by the rules to earn their living by such means as instructing, or training eventers, by being paid to ride other people's horses in events, or by such connected occupations as keeping a livery yard.

Eventing is perhaps one of the most genuinely amateur sports amongst all those included in the Olympic Games, but inevitably some countries do get round the point to some degree, and to prevent the shadow of shamateurism from spreading it would seem logical and fairer further to relax rules that are already stretched.

The other vexed question connected with the Olympics concerns training the team. In the three years prior to Mexico, promising combinations of British riders and horses went to an official Olympic trainer to work before competing in big events. This enabled him to draw equal comparisons, really to get to know the horses, their capabilities and limitations under different conditions of ground and weather, to supervise their training and competing programmes, and eventually to weld the most likely partners into a team over a considerable period of time. Since then, for reasons of economy the British have depended for an Olympic short list of riders and horses solely on the good judgement of the selection committee. And the possibles all train as individuals up to the last few weeks before the Games when they do come under the instruction of one trainer.

Britain does hold a position second to none in the Olympic three-day event records, but competition grows keener with the years and by 1976 the Americans, a looming danger to British prestige, had been under the instruction of a brilliant trainer and working together as the nucleus of a team since 1970.

On the other hand there is a danger in becoming so serious about sport that it is no longer sport, it becomes mixed up with political and over-nationalistic prestige, where the athletes, and the riders, are treated more as gladiators than sportsmen, as in the communist countries.

The future of combined training as a whole must depend, to a degree like most things, on the economic state of the country. But on this score, although horses are expensive items both to obtain and to keep, and the costs rise in direct ratio to the standard of competitor and horse, for the time being combined training in England, the USA and Australia is an ever-expanding sport. In Europe there are seldom more than thirty competitors in the top national championships, at Badminton in 1976 around seventy actually started out of ninety-seven entries, and that is a vast number of riders for the organizers to get through the various phases. In fact a slight drop in numbers might be welcomed. A system for administrating priority entries at other events for those that have to be refused in the spring trials has been operating successfully.

On a wider spectrum, more of the general public are beginning to understand what the sport is about and to take an added interest in it. This began some years ago when success in international competitions brought names of top event riders, and horses, to the fore, and once the technical challenge of providing television coverage at Badminton and Burghley had been met, producers and public alike realized that combined training competitions do make riveting viewing. Princess Anne's wholehearted and successful participation in the sport did much to boost interest throughout the world, and now that she and Mark provide the only top-class husband and wife eventing 'team', the good work continues.

A time may come when the eventing life of the top-liner horses has come to an end and owners, with enforced lower expenditure on leisure, may decide to keep one dual-role horse, instead of having a horse to hunt and another to event. They will expect one animal to cope with both sports, a jack-of-all-trades rather like the officer's charger of times past, and therefore unlikely to be as high-powered as the three-day eventing specialist of today. If this should occur, it would mean a comparable drop in the standard of eventing at the top. This is something that does happen to a degree after each Olympic Games. Neither Badminton nor Burghley are quite as tough in the succeeding years and there is a gradual build-up to prepare for the next Games. A slight overall reduction, even at Olympic standard, might not be a bad thing for the sport. No class of riders form a closer partnership with their horses or are more conscientious in preparing them for what they have to do, than the three-day eventers, but there is a physical and mental limit to what a horse can do, and that cannot be far away from 1976 standards. Although the horse tragedies that marred the spring season of this year had nothing to do with the severity of the competitions concerned, this is something not always understood by the general public. The most competitive-minded rider who is also a knowledgeable horseman would never wish to overface his horse, and knows there is a built-in safeguard against doing so, because it is impossible to make a horse tackle a fence if it does not wish to. The top riders also know that the worst falls occur, not so much because an obstacle is big and tough, but through misjudgement on the part of the rider, or because the horse is unfit or tired. The general public does not know these things and judge by what they see with their own eyes, or read in the papers, and on their verdict rests the good name of the sport, and therefore its future.

So long as people keep horses, and sponsors and organizers continue to give their support, there seems little to fear in the future for those who make one-day horse trials their chosen sport. Combined training is expanding even faster at the lower levels than it is at the top. Every year more riders are coming into a form of competing where the rewards may be more elusive than materialistic, but where there is challenge, a spice of danger, fun and intense satisfaction in striving for the unattainable – perfection in every phase.

Appendix

BHS OFFICIAL HORSE TRIALS

Month	Event and Duration		Classes
March	Crookham, Hants	Two-day	N, I, OI
	Wingerworth, Derbyshire	One-day	N, I
	Ermington, Devon	One-day	N, OI
	Penzance, Cornwall	One-day	N
	Brigstock, Northants	One-day	N, I, A, Junior Trial
	Downlands, Hants	One-day	N, I, A
	Kinlet, Worcs	One-day	I, A
	Rushall, Wilts	One-day	N, I, A
	Corbridge, Northumberland	One-day	N, OI, Junior Trial
	Windsor, Berks	Two-day	N, OI
April	Charterhall, Berwickshire	One-day	N
	Lockerley Hall, Hants	One-day	N, Junior Trial
	Fenton, Northumberland	One-day	N, OI
	BADMINTON THREE-DAY EVENT, Glos.		
	Coakham, Kent	One-day	N
	Pembroke, Dyfed	One-day	N, I
	Portman, Dorset	One-day	N
	Henstridge, Somerset	One-day	N, I, OI
	South of England, Sussex	One-day	N, Junior Trial
	Penrice, Glamorgan	One-day	N
	Wramplingham, Norfolk	One-day	N, OI
	Brougham, Cumbria	One-day	N
	Llanfechain, Powys	Two-day	N, (N, OI two-day)
May	Locko Park, Derbyshire	One-day	N, OI
	Farleigh, Somerset	One-day	N
	Batsford, Glos	One-day	N, I, A
	Sherborne, Dorset	One-day	N, I, OI
	Rudding Park, Yorks	One-day	N, OI
	Bretherton, Lancs	One-day	N, OI
	Wellesbourne, Warwickshire	One-day	N
	TIDWORTH THREE-DAY EVENT, Hants		
	Devonshaw, Clackmannonshire	One-day	N, OI
	Sandhurst, Surrey	One-day	N, OI

	Earl Soham, Suffolk	One-day	N
	Bolton, Lancs	One-day	N
June	BRAMHAM THREE-DAY EVENT, Yorks		
July	Tatton Park, Cheshire	One-day	N
August	Eglinton, Ayrshire	One-day	N, OI
	Wendover, Bucks	One-day	N
	Annick, Ayrshire	One-day	N, OI
	Dauntsey Park, Wilts	Two-day	N, I, OI
	Lockerbie, Dumfriesshire	One-day	N, OI
	Stoneleigh, Warwickshire	One-day	N
	Osberton, Notts	Two-day	N, (OI, Junior Two-day)
	Everdon, Northants	One-day	N
	Claughton, Lancs	One-day	N, OI
	Wilton, Wilts	One-day	N
	Molland, Devon	One-day	N, OI
	Wellesbourne, Warwickshire	One-day	N
	Ingleden Park, Kent	One-day	N, OI
September	Graveley, Herts	One-day	N
	Catterick, Yorks	One-day	N, OI
	Firle Place, Sussex	One-day	N
	East Hanningfield, Essex	One-day	N
	Meriden, Warwickshire	One-day	N, I
	Royal Welsh, Powys	One-day	N
	BURGHLEY THREE-DAY EVENT, Lincs		
	Aberuthven, Perthshire	One-day	N, OI
	Kyre, Worcs	One-day	N, OI
	Bucklebury, Berks	Two-day	N, I, OI
	Caldwell, Yorks	One-day	N, OI
	Cromer, Norfolk	One-day	N
	Taunton Vale, Somerset	One-day	N, OI
	Central Scotland, Perthshire	One-day	N
	Billesdon, Leics	One-day	N
	WYLYE THREE-DAY EVENT, Wilts		
	Pollok Park, Glasgow	Two-day	N
October	Midland Bank Championships at		
	Goodwood, Sussex	Two-day	
	Stokenchurch, Bucks	One-day	N, OI
	Royal Deeside, Aberdeenshire	One-day	N
	Whitton Park, Worcs	One-day	N
	Shipley Park, Derbyshire	One-day	N
	Chatsworth, Derbyshire	One-day	I, A

Fixture list courtesy of BHS Combined Training Group, Kenilworth
Key to classes

A	Advanced	N	Novice
OI	Open Intermediate		
I	Intermediate		

Note: Eridge Trials, mentioned in the book are not held at present.